UKIYOE

IMAGES

OF

UNKNOWN

JAPAN

Published for the
Trustees of the British Museum
by British Museum Publications

UKIYOE

IMAGES

OF

UNKNOWN

JAPAN

edited by

LAWRENCE SMITH

© 1988 The Trustees of the British Museum
Published by British Museum Publications Ltd,
46 Bloomsbury Street, London WC1B 3QQ

Second impression 1989

British Library Cataloguing in Publication Data
Ukiyoe: images of unknown Japan.
  1. Japanese prints, 1600–1868
  I. Smith, Lawrence, *1941–*
769.952

  ISBN 0-7141-1438-3

Designed by Harry Green

Set in Linotron 202 Palatino by
Rowland Phototypesetting Ltd, Bury St Edmunds, Suffolk
and printed in Italy by
Arnoldo Mondadori, Verona

COVER Torii Kiyonaga, *The Bush-Clover Garden*, 1783–4,
woodblock (diptych print). See also p. 81.

PAGES 1–2 Kitagawa Utamaro, *Going down to the East*,
1795–1800, woodblock (triptych print). See also p. 95.

CONTENTS

PREFACE

The British Museum's collection of prints, illustrated books and albums of the *Ukiyoe* School is one of the most comprehensive outside Japan. It includes many items which are no longer found in their country of origin, or are difficult of access there. The state and condition of the prints are also exceptionally fine. It was therefore understandable that the Ukiyoe Society of Japan should wish to include a selection from it in their series of major exhibitions of *Ukiyoe* from non-Japanese collections. The selection was accordingly made by Professor Muneshige Narazaki, Chairman of the Society, and the exhibition took place in the spring of 1985 at the Mori Art Museum in Tokyo and the Nara Prefectural Art Museum, with the support of Asahi Newspapers, Japan Airlines and the Japan Foundation.

This publication is based on the selection which was then made, and which has subsequently been displayed at the Fitzwilliam Museum, Cambridge, and the British Museum itself. The photographs were taken by David Gowers of the British Museum Photographic Service. The colour separations were made in Japan and have been generously given by Asahi Newspapers to make this full colour book possible at a reasonable price.

For the original Japanese catalogue, descriptions of all the exhibits were prepared by scholars from the Ukiyoe Society under the supervision of Professor Narazaki. Mr Shūgō Asano, now of the Chiba City Museum, was particularly active in this work. Those entries form the basis of the picture captions in this book. The short biographies of artists are also edited from the Society's text. The introduction uses, with their permission, information and ideas originally presented by Professor Narazaki and Mr Sadao Kikuchi, President of the Society, in their essays in the Japanese catalogue. They were written, however, for Japanese readers who would know much of the background material which is far from obvious to non-Japanese. A new essay has therefore been written for this different audience, but my debt to the original authors is very great and is here acknowledged. A new glossary has been provided.

In the case of the woodblock books and albums captions have been written using where relevant the descriptions published in my joint work with Mr Jack Hillier, *Japanese Prints: 300 Years of Albums and Books* (British Museum Publications, 1980). As always Mr Hillier has been tireless in his advice, now facilitated by his position as a voluntary staff member of the Department of Japanese Antiquities. Timothy Clark, who has recently joined the Department as an *Ukiyoe* specialist, has made many suggestions and corrections to the text and has contributed much to the value of this book. I acknowledge also help with the first translation of the Japanese text by Rebecca Salter. Elizabeth Foxell and Margaret Robinson have typed numerous versions of the text with good humour, and Deborah Wakeling has been, as always, a punctilious and patient editor.

Finally, I wish to thank the scholar and collector Robert Vergez of Tokyo who first proposed to me in 1984 that the British Museum's *Ukiyoe* collection should be shown in Japan; and most of all Asahi Newspapers who made it possible by their financial support. They have since become one of the British Museum's greatest benefactors. It is pleasing that we were first brought together by the art which is the subject of this book.

LAWRENCE SMITH
*Keeper of Japanese Antiquities,
British Museum*

THE HISTORY OF UKIYOE

The art discussed in this book belonged mainly to the great city of Edo, which was the seat of Government of the Shoguns (military dictators) of the Tokugawa family from 1603 to 1868. These years are called the Edo period. Its artistic origins, however, lay in the ancient city of Kyoto, the cradle of both courtly and bourgeois culture. During most of the Edo period the Shoguns imposed virtual Isolation on the country: almost no Japanese could travel abroad; foreign presence was restricted to Chinese and Dutch traders confined to Nagasaki, occasional diplomatic missions and a few Buddhist monks. In this setting Ukiyoe art grew to maturity.

In January 1657 a great fire in Edo burnt out the central governmental district and many downtown areas. Parts of Edo Castle, the seat of the Shogun, were burnt down and only partly rebuilt. Many shrines and temples were lost, plus 400 chō (small districts) of town houses and 800 chō of the downtown area. The death-toll climbed to 106,046. This led to the establishment of a proper fire service (no. 22), but it was far from the last great Edo fire. The city survived them all, however, and still thrives under its modern name of Tokyo.

Both physical and social changes followed, especially in the outlook of the ruling samurai class. The layout of Edo was altered to isolate shrines and temples and move red-light districts to such areas as Asakusa, away from the areas near the Castle and the residences of the feudal lords. By August 1657 the licensed brothel district, now renamed the New Yoshiwara, was exercising its restored practice of twenty-four-hour business there. The Kabuki theatres too had moved to Kayaba-chō and nearby Sakai-chō. Many people drafted in to rebuild Edo stayed on, and the population was always thereafter rising. Edo's historical division into Yamanote and Shitamachi (uptown and downtown) dates from this period. The red-light districts became pockets of freedom and classlessness within a society strictly codified by the Government. They were described by the authorities as 'bad places', but their inhabitants adopted the gloomy Buddhist word ukiyo (the dark, shifting world of existence) and changed its meaning to the 'Floating World' (of pleasure), turning frivolity into its own virtue. Thus was named Ukiyoe art – 'Pictures of the Floating World' – which became a symbol of the independence and pride of the ever-increasing urban classes.

From then on began the lively publication of critiques of courtesans and actors and other illustrated books about the Floating World. These were done by the ancient woodblock printing technique. In the 1650s woodblock printing began to translate Ukiyoe images, already existing in paintings, into widely available books. Skills developed in Japan for some 1,000 years to carve pages of printed text into woodblocks were now used to print the outline illustrations which were implicit in the technique, but had only sporadically been used for pictures outside China itself, where printing had been born.

One of the earliest illustrators of the Ukiyoe book was Hishikawa Moronobu (c.1618–94), whose earliest dated work appeared in 1672. He was from a family of textile producers and designers, and retained his connections with the world of fashion, which was always one of the great subjects of Ukiyoe. The designs on the kimono continued for over two centuries to be the main point of visual interest in many Ukiyoe prints and books. Moronobu was also a painter and developed a polished, highly finished coloured style suitable for the handscroll and album formats, and devoted mainly to scenes in the New Yoshiwara brothel district. In illustrated books and the slowly emerging separate sheet prints, then restricted to monochrome, it was his achievement to devise a convincing and effective black and white style suitable to the woodblock medium. He published around a hundred picture-books, illustrations to other writers' texts, and about fifty erotic books. The latter type was always a major part of Ukiyoe art, and almost all the artists produced erotica as a matter of course in paintings, prints or books (see book 3). The erotic element was naturally never far away where the subject-matter was the great courtesans and their activities.

In 1687, as Moronobu and Sugimura Jihei (no. 3, book 4) were establishing that typically *Ukiyoe* sense of mystery in the portrayal of beautiful women, Torii Kiyonobu and his father Kiyomoto arrived in Edo to work as artists connected with the popular Kabuki theatre, as they had already done in Osaka. They designed posters and painted billboards, and Kiyonobu turned his hand to printed actor portraits, adapting his style to express the rough, vigorous type of acting known as *aragoto*, pioneered by the actor Ichikawa Danjūrō I (d. 1704). *Aragoto* became the rage of Edo in the 1680s, and has, in the hands of his successors, been a force in Kabuki ever since. The Torii style, based on the bold, energetic lines of painted and printed posters, was adopted by Kiyonobu's colleague Kiyomasu I. To these monochrome prints were sometimes added hand colours, especially yellow and the strong, red lead pigment called *tan* (no. 13). The Torii artists continued to work on Kabuki subjects into the twentieth century, using both the vigorous Edo style and a quieter, subtler manner derived from their origins in the theatre of Osaka and Kyoto.

Kiyonobu also continued Moronobu's good work in creating a viable black and white printed style to depict the subtle sensuality of the great courtesans and other beautiful women. No. 7 is a fine example, even though the subject is in fact a female impersonator (a favourite *Ukiyoe* device). This style was taken up in the monumental and now very rare prints of the Kaigetsudō School, which were never surpassed for grandeur among courtesan portraits. Prints were still relatively unimportant, for the Kaigetsudō artists were more active in the field of hanging-scroll paintings of the same subjects, which survive in greater numbers (no. 5). Yet it was gradually becoming more necessary for *Ukiyoe* painters to become publicised through woodblock prints and books, and these extra large prints seem to have functioned as hanging scrolls for the less than very rich. However, there were a few substantial Edo *Ukiyoe* painters who never entered the print world at all, of whom the most notable was Miyagawa Chōshun (1683–1753).

Single-sheet prints were also rather less important than illustrated books until the decade 1740–50, and it was a designer of black and white book illustrations who caused the next change in *Ukiyoe* style. This was Nishikawa Sukenobu (1671–1750), leader of the school in Kyoto, which was still officially Japan's capital and seat of the Emperor, although politically superseded by Edo since 1603. Sukenobu's style was quieter, more refined than that of Edo *Ukiyoe*, but the great social prestige of Kyoto led to his work's being admired and sold in both cities. There it influenced the pictorial composition of the painter Chōshun.

Sukenobu's most important contribution to Japanese art was the creation of a visual world combining apparent innocence with almost aristocratic polish, elements until then missing in the more red-blooded *Ukiyoe* of Edo, which had tended frankly to acknowledge the non-wifely attractions of the Yoshiwara courtesans. In Sukenobu's hands the women of the licensed districts (for Kyoto had them too) took on the aspect of fresh young girls, complaisant to men in every way, but apparently unsoiled by the demands of their profession. It was a fabrication of great general appeal and became the basis of Harunobu's similar visual world a generation later.

Sukenobu's second great contribution to *Ukiyoe* style has less often been acknowledged. He perfected a method of placing figures in a recognisable urban scene, indoors or out, with a sense of spatial relationship between foreground, middle ground and, where appropriate, background. This can best be seen in his most famous book, 'Critical Studies of One Hundred Women' (1723), one of the last *Ukiyoe* masterpieces in simple black and white (book 7). Each illustration was produced by cutting only one block in relief and printing it with *sumi* (black ink). By now that had become a well-understood, effective and relatively cheap technique. In this book he covers the whole social spectrum of Japanese women with a freedom which must have been fascinatingly attractive to people who in reality lived in a society divided by Government decree into the four official classes of samurai, farmer, artisan and merchant, plus other officially recognised groupings such as the court nobility in Kyoto and Buddhist and Shintō priests. In the classless society of the Floating World some (and eventually all) of these could be transcended. Sukenobu's pictorial construction gave a sense of physical connection and intimate scale which had hardly existed before. It too was to be taken up by many later artists, especially Harunobu.

This development owed something to European art, known mostly through European engravings imported through the Dutch trading post at Nagasaki. Through them *Ukiyoe* artists in the first half of the eighteenth century learned to organise a scene linked by lines or connecting objects, and to adopt a lower viewpoint than that of much traditional Japanese art. It was a confirmation of tendencies they had been struggling towards since the days of Moronobu. To understand this process one must examine the ancient, native tradition of painting in the style called *Yamatoe*. Some of its characteristics can be seen in the Buddhist print (no. 4), the scenes of rural life by Kiyonobu and Kiyomasu (nos 14–15) and the stylistically conservative Sumiyoshi School painted scrolls of popular life in Ueno and Asakusa (nos 48–9). The last are interesting to compare with the young Sukenobu's exactly contemporary influential new works. In these *Yamatoe* works the artists have tried to show groups of people in relationship to each other but have been able to do it only from a distance and from above. The setting therefore feels confined by the artificial device of hovering above the scene, and depth too relies on the artificial distance placed between the viewer and the scene. This was true of Moronobu's painted handscrolls, but in his prints and books he began to achieve a sense of intimacy between his figures and with the beholder by bringing down the point of view and creating a limited sense of space behind them. It can be seen in his cherry-viewing scene (no. 1), which is already in some respects visually more sophisticated than the elaborate, later handscroll on the same subject (no. 48); that remains true to *Yamatoe* traditions. Its impact is accordingly one of joyous detail rather than tight construction.

Sukenobu brought the viewpoint down still lower. When this happened, it gave new life to the old *Yamatoe* painting tradition of drawing the lines of, for example, buildings at a slant of forty-five degrees (no. 2, book 3). This technique was originally developed to minimise the clumsiness of parallel lines (often used for the interiors of houses, or verandas) without the use of perspective, then unknown to artists. In that sense placing the lines on a slant was a holding-operation. Sukenobu made it a vivid way of suggesting that space was spreading in all directions, including and embracing the viewer (book 7). Indeed, the low, slanted view became one of the most favoured *Ukiyoe* compositional techniques after Sukenobu and was widely used by Harunobu, Koryūsai, Shumman and Eishi, and even later artists. Its finest expression, one might suggest, was in the dazzlingly inventive picture-book 'A Mirror of Beautiful Women of the Green Houses Compared' by Shunshō and Shigemasa (book 12). Obviously one of the advantages of this way of suggesting an interior was its power to hint at a wider context without having to depict it in detail.

Yet a sense of deep space had already long existed in the landscape method of the Kanō School, official painters to the Shoguns, whose methods were derived from Chinese landscape styles of much earlier periods. One of their devices used a strongly defined foreground to create a sense of deep, misty space behind it. Toriyama Sekien's book 'Sekien's Picture-album' (1774) is a fine example, translated into the woodblock medium, of just that device (book 15). The women of Ōhara, carrying their faggots on their heads, cross a stream. What is beyond can only be sensed but suggests depth. Sekien was a Kanō-trained artist and the teacher of Utamaro, who also used this technique, notably in his riverside scene (no. 81).

While Sukenobu extended the range of *Ukiyoe*, it was still used mostly for indoor and street scenes. In some of his books he also used a telling visual technique which had existed since the art of the Floating World was born in the mid-seventeenth century. Its essence – simple, but forcible and flexible – was the placing of one or more figures on no background at all. It was used originally in hanging scrolls and handscrolls on paper or silk, the classic formats of Japanese painting. It was the usual method of the Kaigetsudō painters and was reproduced in their prints, such as no. 5 where we see the great courtesan placed in pure space. Only her bare feet show she is indoors. We have to guess the rest. We can do so, as could the first buyers of the prints, because she is placed closely in front of us. The early *Ukiyoe* hanging scrolls of beautiful women had already perfected this close-up, low viewpoint construction. It was one of the glories of the school, and remained so through to the nineteenth century. Sukenobu used it most effectively in his 'Picture-book of Mount Asaka' (book 8) of 1739. His touching groups of two or three women with men or children set a standard until late in the century. This tradition can still be seen in Eishi's great print (*c*.1795) of the courtesan Nakagawa with two apprentices (no. 119). There the artist uses a table and a scroll to link the figures, but there is no background at all. Even later, Hokkei continues the tradition in his fine painting of a mother and child (no. 178) of *c*.1835, using domestic objects to suggest a specific indoor setting.

These subtleties, it seems, were not vivid enough for the increasingly mass public for books and sheet prints. They wanted concrete reminders of the brilliant, entertaining, fashionable and crowded Floating World they spent their money in – the theatres, tea-houses, great brothels, shops, stalls, wrestling tournaments, tourist temples and picnic spots. In the decade 1740–50 publishers sought innovations to satisfy this demand, essentially for novelty. It was most vigorously met by the publisher and artist Okumura Masanobu (1681–1764), usually the quickest to create or follow new ideas. He began with black and white courtesan portraits and Kabuki theatre scenes in his extreme youth, learned in the school of Kiyonobu. He progressed to the cleverly handled multi-sheet set of the Korean embassy procession of 1711 (no. 25) which enlivens a visually monotonous subject by turning it into a long handscroll issued in sections. He then moved to a more delicate style of female portraiture influenced by Sukenobu. In no. 26 he uses such a style to depict an actor in a female part but employs a much larger format imitating a painted hanging scroll. Large prints had been rarely issued, because the handmade paper for printing came in smaller sheets which had to be

pasted up into larger pieces, and also because large enough printing blocks (cut with the grain) were difficult to obtain from the most suitable tree, the northern cherry. By now, though, townsmen of means were apparently demanding and paying for these substitute paintings in the hanging-scroll format. They were sometimes mounted with paper surrounds and a hanging cord so that they could actually be used as such.

Masanobu's most noticeable innovations came in the fields of style and technique. In style he was the most active designer of the 'perspective prints' in which the strict rules of recession to a vanishing-point, as learned from Dutch engravings, were used tellingly for the first time to represent crowded interiors (nos 27–8). The natural subjects were the Edo Kabuki theatres, of which we get our first convincing interior glimpse in these *ukie*. Until then interior scenes had used native *Yamatoe* techniques, either looking from above as if the roof was not there, or omitting any background except for a few indicators left as clues. Other 'perspective pictures' are illustrated in nos 37, 46 and 47. They had a vogue in the decade 1740–50, when they must have seemed excitingly up to date; indeed, their titles often point out that they *are* perspective prints in case any of the customers should miss the fact. The *ukie* technique was later extended to crowded outside events, such as the scenes by Katsukawa Shun'ei of a Sumō wrestling tournament and a street festival (nos 131–2). These scenes, nevertheless, sometimes retained the native tendency to make more important figures unnaturally bigger than others; the results might then be exotic rather than convincing (no. 132). Subtler artists – Kiyonaga and Utamaro in townscape, Hokusai and Hiroshige in townscape, landscape and seascape – integrated perspective into a quieter and more satisfying hybrid style. Compared with the perspective scenes of Masanobu, Hiroshige's ferry scene (no. 183), for example, looks almost carelessly assured in its composition. It is also, one must remember, nearly a century later.

To achieve such results the possibilities of full colour printing, among other things, had to be developed and thoroughly understood. Until around 1740 any colour in *Ukiyoe* prints had to be added by hand, an expensive and not always satisfactory process, although the results could be charming (as in no. 7 by Kiyonobu) or quietly sumptuous (as in no. 31 by Shigenaga). Colours were restricted mainly to yellows, purples, oranges and reds, with applied metal or mineral dusts, or lacquered effects achieved by mixing glue with black ink. Masanobu used all of these, but jumped at the chance to exploit this traditional East Asian use of symbolically selective colour through the woodblock medium. Full colour printing had flourished in China since the fifteenth century and had been known in Japan since the mid-seventeenth, but economics and lack of sure technique had held back its use. The time was now ripe, and Edo printers and publishers took the step of adding two colour blocks, one pink and one green, to the black key-block. This necessitated only one extra block, since one side could be carved with the pink areas and one with the green. The colours were vegetable dyes which would be thoroughly water-soluble and transfer well from the block to the paper. Whoever actually did this first, it was, as usual, Masanobu who exploited it most (no. 29).

These *benizurie* ('pictures printed in pink *beni* dye') had a vogue of only about twenty years but they resulted in designs of great elegance, some of which rank among the finest *Ukiyoe* prints (nos 19, 20 and 35). Unluckily, these dyes fade over the centuries, and only a few, such as those illustrated here, retain some of their former splendour. No. 38, by Mangetsudō, gives the most vivid idea of their original freshness. It was soon realised that overprinting the two colours could result in a third colour of a greyish-violet hue. It can be seen in details of the dress of the geisha (entertainer) in no. 29 by Masanobu. By around 1760 a few extra colours were sometimes printed. A greater confidence entered the *Ukiyoe* print. Actors and beautiful women alike were portrayed with a new ease and grace, as in Kiyomitsu's Kabuki subjects (nos 39–40). The influence of Sukenobu was everywhere, enhanced by the new expressiveness in printing techniques, which now seemed better able to translate the individual flavour of each artist into the woodblock medium.

Since the mid-seventeenth century the sheet print had been far from the dominant *Ukiyoe* form. The rich ordered paintings, the less rich bought illustrated books; the sheet print was not yet the main product of the publisher. Then (traditionally in 1764) was 'born' the full colour print which ever after dominated the field and which nearly a century later was to carry *Ukiyoe* to a Western world then ready to applaud it. As we have seen, printing in several colours had been advancing, but expense had prevented general production for sale. In the 1750s and 60s groups of amateur poets in Edo began to commission illustrated calendars to exchange at the New Year. The complex lunar calendar divided the year into twelve, sometimes thirteen months, some short and some long, and their combinations varied every year. Calendars giving all the necessary information thus became desirable. Two later examples of picture calendars by Shiba Kōkan are reproduced in nos 62 and 63.

These wealthy poetry groups were able to commission illustrated calendars printed in many colours. The first sets, it is recorded, were produced for the New Year of 1765, signed by the poets who had commissioned them, and made such a stir that the publisher Shōkakudō bought the carved blocks (in other words, the copyright) for the following year's calendar illustrations and reissued them unsigned. It shortly became known that Suzuki Harunobu (1724–70), was the designer of some of the best, and his signature then began to appear on the many hundreds of designs which he thenceforth continued to produce.

These prints became known as *azuma nishikie* – 'brocade pictures from the East', that is, from Edo. The term *nishikie* has been used ever since in Japan for the full colour prints of the *Ukiyoe* School. It was as if the *Ukiyoe* print had grown up almost overnight, and with it Harunobu himself, until then a minor painter and designer of book illustrations. He developed from the beginning the design possibilities of the new medium, and his work at once made the sheet print the dominant form, no longer a second-best to painting but a self-confident rival to it. The Floating World had always been an intensely colourful one – of fashion, festivals, shops, the extrovert Kabuki and puppet theatres –

but now at last it could express itself fully in its own popular and buyable art-form.

To understand how much art, skill and labour went into a colour print and how co-operative a venture it was it is necessary to describe how it was made. The artist produced a fairly free design in ink; usually the colour was simply indicated by written symbols, or sometimes with a few indicative washes of pigment. It was drawn up carefully by a pupil, or by an employee of the publisher or printer, on thin paper – this was the *hanshitae*. Three unused *hanshitae* for prints by Hokusai are reproduced in nos 169–71. It was then pasted face-down on to a carefully chosen and seasoned thin block of cherry wood, cut with the grain. These blocks were so expensive that they were sometimes planed down after one use and recut. The blockmaker would then cut round the lines and larger areas of black shown in the *hanshitae*, leaving them in relief. From this key-block preliminary black and white impressions could be taken, still resembling the uncoloured prints of earlier periods, such as no. 5. By using these impressions in turn as *hanshitae* it was possible to carve separate blocks in relief with the areas for each colour. Each of these had, normally, to be on a separate surface, so every two colours made necessary an extra block, assuming both sides were used. The blockmaker's skill at this point was crucial to the fineness of the final effect.

The printing could now begin. First, the key-block was printed by wiping the areas in relief with black ink, placing the dampened handmade paper on it, and rubbing the back with a pad. No press was used. When a chosen number of these had dried, the first colour was printed on each sheet, then each colour in turn. It was here that the skill of the printer came into play. He had to wipe the colour on to the block to produce exactly the effect needed, either dense and brilliant as in Sharaku's actor portraits (nos 135–49) or light and delicately shaded-off, as in the gradations of purple on the outer robes in Eishi's print of Takikawa (no. 118). He had to print the colours in exact registration with the key-block and with each other, a problem which had, because of the expense in time and materials needed to solve it, held up the full colour print in Japan for some eighty years. The technique itself was simple, consisting of a right-angled notch cut into one corner of the block, into which the corner of the paper slotted; a line in relief on one of the sides ensured the paper stayed straight. Fine results depended on very accurate cutting of both block and paper and the dexterity, sensitivity and experience of the printer.

Using this process different impressions could vary considerably, and each impression must in fact differ minutely. Printers could experiment deliberately with effects from the same blocks, and quite different colours might be used for alternative impressions (nos 181–2). Later impressions might be taken literally generations later by successors of the original publishers, who no longer knew the intentions of the artist or printers, or who in some cases lacked the skill or standards of their forebears. Key-blocks would deteriorate, slowly at first, but losing much of their sharpness as they approached the 10,000 impressions which were about the reasonable limit. No. 159 illustrates a copy of Eisen's view of Oiwake in relatively worn condition and with imperfect registration. No. 161, a view of the bridge at Nojiri by the same artist, shows far greater finesse and accuracy. Only the most successful designs were printed in thousands; others would be erased, presumably if the first batch did not sell well, so that the blocks could be reused. The number of *nishikie* which could be printed by one man in one day was only hundreds, and in many cases that may have been the complete edition. It is not surprising that only one or two copies of certain prints survive to the present day. We know that some, perhaps many, have not survived at all. Utamaro's river scene (no. 81) is apparently a unique survivor.

On these skills depended the flowering of the colour print under Harunobu's leadership. As a pupil of Sukenobu, his style owes much to the earlier master's, but the introduction of colour gives a new confidence which never afterwards left the sheet print. Looking at these harmoniously coloured prints, still fresh in effect after two centuries in spite of the gradual fading of the dyes, it is easy to understand the excitement they caused. Yet they are based on the *Yamatoe* tradition of simple, thin outline filled in with more or less flat colour, and with no attempt to suggest light and shade. They are a revival of the ancient *Yamatoe* tradition in a new urban form.

Harunobu considered himself literally a *Yamatoe* artist, scornful of the vulgarities of the Kabuki theatre (which was, it might be retorted, the true essence of the Floating World). His version of *Ukiyoe* was dreamy, elegant, almost insubstantial, showing great affinities with the courtly literature and art of Kyoto, which had flourished continuously since the tenth century. Where that art had centred on courtly lovers of almost unbelievable reticence and refinement, Harunobu substituted, by a most piquant reversal, the prostitutes of the New Yoshiwara, the hostesses of the fashionable Edo tea-houses and their clients of the merchant and samurai classes. His prints often compare these to the courtly heroes and heroines of the past, accompanied by poems from classical literature written on bands of cloud and mist drifting across the picture, again copying *Yamatoe* practice (no. 53). He thus played to the social pretensions of the newly rich Edo and Osaka merchants and financiers, who were enthusiastic patrons of the New Yoshiwara and of the arts of the Floating World. He adopted Sukenobu's disarmingly innocent view of what was, after all, a fiercely demanding, professional world based on exploitation on all sides, and made it doubly attractive. His often pungent double meanings are elegantly concealed with a subtle evasiveness rarely again found in *Ukiyoe*.

Even his faces have that anonymity which the courtly painting tradition demanded, sketched in with two lines for eyes, two for eyebrows, one hook for a nose, and a tiny bud for a mouth. In his portrait of an actual court poetess of the ninth century, Ono no Komachi (no. 55), these conventions are literally observed; but compared with her inhibitingly stiff, many-layered court dress, how relaxed, unfettered, almost undressed Harunobu's courtesans and waitresses seem (no. 56)!

Harunobu had successfully merged classical ideas of the most desirable qualities in a woman with different attitudes of freedom and availability (at a price) from the Floating World itself. Courtly ideals valued extreme reticence and good taste; the refined woman should communicate that peculiarly Japanese sense of loneliness, the transience of things, known as *mono no aware*. Harunobu and his master Sukenobu both introduced into *Ukiyoe* just that sense of nostalgic melancholy and loneliness, especially in their treatment of women. The melancholy courtesan in no. 51 is a good example. Such feelings, constantly expressed in poetry as well as art, found an echo in the very word *ukiyo* with its original sense of the 'dark world' which passes away; but they do not make their full appearance in *Ukiyoe* until Sukenobu and Harunobu. They, too, devised a purely pictorial expression of the ideal woman of the Floating World. This ideal portrayal had already been described eighty years earlier in the texts of Moronobu's picture-books, which mention the qualities of finely detailed depiction, slenderness, tenderness, prettiness and gracefulness. Those terms, strangely, seem more accurately to define Harunobu's women three generations later, and those of his followers Koryūsai and the young Shunshō.

From this point of balance the women of *Ukiyoe* prints gradually became, in the next generation, grander and more overdressed, certainly more formidable and much more expensive. It is not surprising that Harunobu's age has long been regarded in Japan and in the West as a lost world of near-innocence. It is, of course, an illusion of innocence.

The connection with medieval courtly culture was of great importance for the 'Golden Age' of *Ukiyoe*, which began with the full colour print and continued until the end of the century. Frequent references to the aristocratic poets and poetesses of the past show a society where all was not what it seemed, where the natural upward aspirations of a whole class of townsmen could be met only in those officially cut-off and unreal islands which were the licensed quarters of prostitution. Here, the great houses of courtesans (no. 46, book 19) became latter-day images of the palaces of Kyoto, centres of elegance, places for poets, artists and novelists to meet each other in the company of supremely elegant women. The top-ranked courtesans, called *oiran* in Edo, became the heroines of this world, just as the ladies of the medieval court had been in their own special, almost secret world. Like them, the *oiran* needed above all literary skills as well as a wide range of informed conversation.

These preoccupations led to the frequent use of *mitatee* – 'travesty pictures'. Three examples, dated 1771–2, 1784 and *c*.1790 show very clearly how these worked. The first, by Kōkan (no. 61), is itself a parody of the style of Harunobu. It shows a scene on the upper floor of a brothel, overlooking the 'Japan Embankment' (*Nihon-tsutsumi*) which led across marshland to the New Yoshiwara. A client is attended by a courtesan who is cleaning his ears while he idly looks at a sheet print signed 'Harunobu', showing the celebrated tea-house hostess Osen at her tea-stall at the Kasamori Inari shrine. The courtesan's apprentice is herself pensively preparing tea. The fanning of the flames under the tea-kettle with a paper handkerchief has obvious sexual allusion.

There is much more to it, however, than this. The title of the print is *Komachi Amagoi* ('Komachi praying for rain'). Ono no Komachi was a ninth-century court lady of great beauty, and the most famous of Japan's poetesses. Her melancholy poems about her own unrequited love, her cruel treatment of those in love with her, and the legends of her tragic decline into destitute old age struck to the heart of Japanese sensibilities, and at no time more deeply than in the New Yoshiwara with its beauties made almost unattainable by their prices. Komachi was asked to deliver the country from a drought and did so by composing the poem printed at the top of the picture. It can be translated: 'Even if this is the land of the Sun's origin it is burning us; is it not also below the rain?' Outside the shutters, on the allusively named 'Japan Embankment', is a figure hurrying through the rain, a reference to Komachi's lover Fukakusa no Shōshō, whom she ordered to visit her house on a hundred successive nights in whatever weather and to make a notch on her door each time to prove it. He died in the snow on the hundredth night. We can speculate that this also refers to the popularity of a particular courtesan, a latter-day Komachi courted by all. These are all very literary references.

A set of seven prints by Kitao Masanobu (1784), issued originally as an album, has the title 'A Mirror Comparing the Handwriting of New and Beautiful Courtesans of the Yoshiwara'. In these prints, which set a new standard of statuesque elegance in *Ukiyoe*, the courtesans are dressed with an elaboration recalling in spirit, if not detail, the medieval Kyoto court. They are presented in pairs, reading or writing, while their calligraphic style is reproduced in the poems printed above them. In the page illustrated here (book 19) Nanasato is even shown with long, loose hair in semi-courtly style (although a court lady would not have wooden hairpins like these). Her outer garment is decorated with some of the symbols traditionally used to number the fifty-four chapters of 'The Tale of Genji', Japan's most celebrated medieval novel of courtly love. For travesties of *Genji* itself see nos 114–15 by Eishi. In no. 116 he combines three poems from the 'Tales of Ise' classic in modern dress. Edo townswomen are shown engaged in the literacy pursuits of a court culture far distant in time and place.

The third example is Utamaro's two-sheet print (no. 85), *A travesty of the 'Six Poets'* (*c*.1790). Six of the most celebrated professional beauties of the day are dressed in their current fashions, but in the attitudes of the 'Six Poetic Immortals' (*Rokkasen*) of the ninth century, known by all educated Japanese. The standing figure and the most overtly beautiful is Hanaōgi as Ono no Komachi. The clouds above them are luxuriously enhanced with powdered mica, on which are printed six *kyōka* (comic verse), by contemporary poets, referring to the women's charms.

The origin of the full colour print in small calendar prints left its mark in smallness of scale and delicacy of printing. Specially thick paper allowed also for embossed effects, as in the portrait of Ono no Komachi (no. 55). For the first few years this feeling of restrained luxury prevailed, but from the late 1760s began a natural movement towards greater scale, wider popularity and hence bigger profits. It was seen first in the *hashirae* (pillar pictures) especially favoured by Koryūsai (nos 66–71). These tall, very narrow prints could be hung or pasted up on the wooden posts of a

Japanese building. They were sometimes mounted as hanging scrolls in cheap paper mounts. Apart from these pillar pictures and the earlier *kakemonoe* (hanging-scroll pictures), there is no evidence that *Ukiyoe* prints were treated as more than ephemera to look at briefly (as in no. 61) and put away in a folder.

The early pillar prints retained the delicate, almost petite figures of Harunobu. However, the mood of the period in Edo was expansive, as society increasingly recovered from the Government reforms and austerities of the Kyōhō Era (1716–35). Print formats and the figures shown in them began to expand into the dimensions which came to be accepted as the norm. The pioneers of this movement were Koryūsai and Shunshō, both of whom started their work under the spell of Harunobu. In Koryūsai's album of courtesan portraits (book 16), published in 1777, the beauties are already taller and haughtier, their clothing is becoming more ornate, and the hairstyles heavier and more cluttered with wooden hairpins and combs. The same tendencies are seen in 1776 in the great picture-book by Shunshō and Shigemasa celebrating the courtesans of the *Seirō* ('Green Houses', a term for the grandest Yoshiwara brothels), through the four seasons (book 12). At the same period artists and publishers gradually increased the single-sheet print to medium dimensions of approximately 320 × 220 mm, as in no. 125. In 1784 Masanobu's album discussed above produced for the first time full colour printed *bijinga* (pictures of beautiful women) in the large format known as *ōban*, approximately 350 × 250 mm. This was such a success that the prints were issued separately and soon became the normal size expected. Most of the later prints reproduced in this book, from no. 74 onwards, are in that format or multiples of it.

The other great preoccupation of the Floating World culture was the Kabuki theatre. In the 1770s Shunshō and Ippitsusai Bunchō found a way of matching the distracting splendour of the new colours by focusing attention on the actor's face and his range of expressions. There is a tendency to take more interest in the actor's personality and private life, encouraged by the growth in the later

eighteenth century of enthusiastic supporters' clubs for individual players. No. 125 is an example of Shunshō's actor *nigaoe* (portrait pictures) done in the traditional full-length pose. *Ehon Butai Ōgi* (book 14), published in 1770, was more radical. In it Shunshō and Bunchō reproduced actors' faces with greater point and precision than ever before, and also showed them half-length, a convention almost never previously used in *Ukiyoe*. The effect was to bring the actor closer to the viewer and therefore make him much more vivid. This convention was used later in the actor portraits of Tōshūsai Sharaku (nos 135–49), which have never been surpassed in Japanese art for their combination of sheer force of design with psychological penetration.

To this tradition too belong the half-length portraits of beautiful women by Utamaro (nos 89–91). With Sharaku's work they mark the culmination of the Floating World spirit, in which people as individuals, rather than as components of an interdependent society, hold the centre of the stage. They must have been seen as a successful protest at a Government always suspicious of independent ways of life and thought, and ever ready to crack down on the New Yoshiwara, the theatres and the publishers. In 1790, in fact, a new Government campaign of austerity and Confucian morality included an order for the censoring of books and prints by representatives of the publishers themselves. This was to help produce in the following years a change in the mood of *Ukiyoe*, and to end the so-called 'Golden Age'.

What were the characteristics of this greatest period of the *Ukiyoe* print? Some have already been mentioned – the emergence of full colour printing, of assured design and printing techniques, of formats specific to the sheet print, of a growing and well-informed market. Others were the relative freedom of the regime in the generation before 1790, the spread downwards of wealth, the dominance of the publisher Tsutaya Jūsaburō, the expansion of pictorial technique by the artist Torii Kiyonaga, and not least the genius of Sharaku and of *Ukiyoe*'s greatest master, Kitagawa Utamaro (1753–1806).

Kiyonaga greatly increased the impact of his human figures by investing them with a new, relaxed dignity (nos 74–80 and cover). This was enhanced by the easy splendour of the textiles worn by his subjects – people, it should be noted, from several levels of Edo society – and simply by increasing their height. Secondly he brought the print fully into the open air with a detailed sense of place (nos 75, 77), benefiting from experiments with Western-style perspective and foreground – background construction by artists such as Shiba Kōkan (no. 64, which is actually an etching) and Utagawa Toyoharu (nos 150, 152). Compared with their work, though, Kiyonaga's open-air scenes have a relaxed grace which results from the total fusion of well-learned lessons into the pure *Ukiyoe* style. This was an important change, for it provided a ready-made style for the major landscape artists of the period after 1830.

His third innovation was to extend his compositions across two and three sheets, a reflection of the broadening outlook of the townsmen who were the buying public of *Ukiyoe*. Multi-sheet compositions had sometimes been done before (see no. 43) but not to produce such wide and connected landscape effects and certainly not to accommodate a change of style. In these multi-sheet compositions (nos 74–7) Kiyonaga supplied the woodblock print's true alternative to the long painted handscroll and thus finally altered the tendency to vertical composition which was the inheritance of the hanging-scroll tradition. The question of how sets of two or more connecting prints were looked at remains unanswered. Many that survive did so because they were made up into folding albums or even actual handscrolls.

The presiding genius of the Golden Age was the publisher Tsutaya Jūsaburō (d. 1797), a man born in the Yoshiwara, widely cultured, with immensely high standards and a talent for inspiring artists and printers. He co-published as early as 1776 Shunshō's and Shigemasa's sumptuous Yoshiwara survey (book 12), and his passion for elegant design and the best possible printing was maintained through all his subsequent ventures. Many of the abiding achievements of the period are due to his supervision, including the great *kyōka* verse anthologies illustrated by Shumman, Utamaro and others; the actor prints of Sharaku; and the sheet prints of Utamaro himself. The anthologies are

specially important, including some of the most delicately printed compositions of the *Ukiyoe* School. The studies of birds, flowers, insects and shells, mainly by Utamaro, went far beyond the traditional scope of Floating World art (books 20, 23–4). Since the time of the exclusive poetry clubs which gave birth to the full colour print, urban society in Japan had become increasingly sophisticated and now expected more than courtesans and actors. Poetry was almost universally cultivated, and the Edo societies which specialised in the light verse called *kyōka* had high status. Their members might double as artists and poets, among whom Utamaro and Kubota Shumman were the most notable. The traditional number of illustrations in the albums was five, and their connection with the subject of the verse might be tenuous, although never entirely irrelevant.

Utamaro has been primarily admired, however, for his dazzling sheet prints, considered by many commentators as the finest graphic work of the Floating World. He took the large, relaxed, almost stately compositional methods of Kiyonaga and invested them with unusually direct emotional impact and psychological insight. Utamaro was fascinated by women as human beings, a trait not often found in *Ukiyoe* artists. He was fascinated by sexual passion, as contrasted with the sexual activity which featured obsessively in the vast erotic output of *Ukiyoe*. He was moved by the emotions of lovers, as represented so powerfully in his grand and dignified print of the eloping lovers Umegawa and Chūbei (no. 99). His male figures correspond closely to his image of himself as elegant, haughty, intense (no. 93). These ingredients give an electricity to his work which has been felt ever since. Like Sharaku's actor portraits, the enigmas under the surface continue to grip the attention.

The death of Tsutaya in 1797 left no obvious successor to maintain his standards. Sharaku had already ended his extremely brief career as a print artist. Utamaro's work shows a lessening of intensity at this time, and his rival Hosoda Eishi soon after gave up print-designing to concentrate on painting. The regulations of 1790 banning erotic works, discouraging overt luxury, and imposing censorship had by about 1805 taken considerable effect, understandably since a number of artists and writers, including Utamaro, had been condemned to periods of house arrest for flouting them. In contrast the ever-increasing real prosperity of the people, in spite of the gloomy stance of the Government, pushed the market for prints down to a lower social level. Artistic taste and standards of printing were likely to change as a result. That same rise in income similarly pushed the older-established *Ukiyoe* patrons and their artists socially upwards into a wider appreciation of older or more prestigious painting styles.

For these and other reasons there is a clear change of mood around the beginning of the nineteenth century. One result was the flowering of prints known as *surimono*. The term simply means 'printed matter' and refers to prints of especially delicate quality done on thick paper, to be used as greeting cards or to commemorate particular events. Their best period was the first third of the century (nos 188–200). They used a restrained palette, embossing of the paper, and often metal leaf, metal dust and mica. Like their ancestors, the calendar prints and *kyōka* albums, they tended to avoid direct reference to the headier aspects of the Yoshiwara. Their use of poetry was general, and one of their best designers was Shumman, himself a leading poet. Another was the many-sided Katsushika Hokusai (1760–1849). Both, significantly, had worked with Tsutaya. By now *surimono* were also designed by artists of other schools. The *Ukiyoe* style was fast losing its once near monopoly of graphic art.

The great figure of the last decades before 'unknown Japan' was opened up was Hokusai, who ranks with Utamaro and Sharaku as one of the major personalities of *Ukiyoe*. Although the beginnings of his long career lay in the Floating World, he can only partly be called a *Ukiyoe* artist. A prolific painter and obsessive sketcher, he also produced a great quantity of illustrations to books, especially those of the novelist Kyokutei Bakin (1767–1848), with a wide range of subjects. He is best known, however, for the landscape series developed in his comparative old age, especially 'Thirty-six Views of Mount Fuji', in which he established the pure landscape as a valid form for the sheet print (no. 172). There he first used Prussian blue, originally a difficult-to-obtain European product, for which a new Chinese source became available in the 1820s. With this strong, unfading blue he could depict sky and water effectively. He introduced European elements (including a coloured sky) as well as Chinese and traditional Japanese devices, merging them into a forceful style which is unmistakably his. Hokusai was and has remained a popular hero in Japan. As such, he is of great significance as a precursor of the less codified social system which succeeded that of the Edo period.

The new landscapes appealed to townsmen who now travelled more widely, and the townscapes to countrymen who visited Edo, Kyoto and Osaka. Andō Hiroshige (1797–1858) took up the new form and gave it a poetic delicacy owing much to the Maruyama-Shijō School of painting which was by then beginning to dominate artistic circles. He and his studio produced many thousands of designs in innumerable series; many continued to be reprinted in ever-inferior batches through the century. Only a fine, early impression, such as *Seba* (no. 184) can give a proper idea of his considerable skill as a landscapist. It was his later landscape series, especially 'One Hundred Views of Edo', which were on sale in Japan when the Isolation policy was ended in 1853 by the arrival of the American Mission.

Also plentifully available at that time were the heavily pigmented prints of the prolific Utagawa School (nos 162–3). They carried on into the late Edo period and beyond the traditional themes of beautiful women and the Kabuki theatre, producing very high numbers of designs for a seemingly insatiable public. Printing skills remained potentially as good as ever but were often obscured by the strong, often violent colours favoured by the Utagawa artists. Their most important master was Utagawa Toyokuni (1769–1825), who even in the late eighteenth century was beginning to favour a more sombre range of colours (nos 155–6), but at that time with no loss of refinement. In fact, its purpose was the reverse, to introduce into *Ukiyoe* a more astringent, upper-class taste. However, the use of Prussian blue after 1830 produced a

17

thickening of the palette which clearly appealed to the uninhibited zest of late Edo popular culture. The women, too, seem to go down-market. The well-proportioned faces of Utamaro, Kiyonaga and Eishi, which aimed almost literally at a sense of nobility, gave way in the later works of Toyokuni, to a longer, sharp-jawed, concentrated, predatory face (see no. 158). It became the typical face of this whole numerous school and is constantly found in the works of the enormously prolific Utagawa Kunisada (1786–1864). His prints are found more commonly than any other artist's in collections outside Japan, and were exported in large numbers in the later nineteenth century. In no. 162, for example, his women are full of energy, ready for action, the reverse of retiring. With the end of the submissive woman, the days of the Floating World itself were numbered.

The Utagawa School had to plot a careful course through the censor's danger-marks – the residual effects of the Kansei Reforms, and the new Tempō Reforms (1841–3) which further attacked unlicensed prostitution, luxury goods and frivolous works of art and literature. One of the objectives of the Tempō Reforms was to improve morale and the military spirit, as the consciousness of the foreign threat to the long Isolation grew ever more uneasy. The Utagawa School complied by issuing prints illustrating the virtues. No. 163 by Kuniyoshi is such a print, but obviously its main interest to the buyer was still the beauty of the women and their apparel. The encouragement of things military led to the outburst of prints of heroic subjects from Japan's past, especially those by Utagawa Kuniyoshi (1797–1861). Strictly speaking, these have no spiritual connection with the Floating World, but nearly two centuries of *Ukiyoe* prints had developed the design skills, the formats and the printing techniques which made them possible, and their artists were drawn from the Utagawa School (nos 164–5). As such, they are the last of the many products of the ever-fertile soil of that most ambiguously named 'Floating World'.

The appreciation and collecting of Ukiyoe in Europe, Britain and the British Museum

The art of *Ukiyoe* – 'Pictures of the Floating World' – first widely introduced Westerners to the pictorial arts of Japan in the mid-nineteenth century at the very time that their incursions were contributing to the end of the enclosed world which produced it. To be precise, it was in 1853 that Commander Perry arrived in Edo Bay to negotiate with the Government of Japan on behalf of the USA. This proved, after some fifty years of unsuccessful tries by various Western nations to do the same, to be the end of the policy of *sakoku* – 'the secluded country' – which had continued since 1633. When Perry arrived, prints such as Hiroshige's landscapes and townscapes (nos 179–87) and the extravaganzas of the Utagawa School (nos 162–5) were on sale in the streets of Edo – the city which in 1868 was to become Tokyo. It was these new and, in the Japanese context, still fashionable prints which were brought back to the Western world at that time. It is important to remember that they were then *contemporary* prints.

Until then Western knowledge of Japanese material culture had been for long restricted very largely to export porcelains and lacquers, made in a taste partly Japanese, partly Chinese and partly European. They were exported from Nagasaki, where officers of the Dutch East India Company, in small numbers, were from 1641 the only exceptions to the ban on Europeans.

Devoted to commerce, pledged to make no attempt to preach Christianity in Japan, these generally unimaginative traders were a far cry from the Jesuits and Franciscans of the preceding century, many of whom had, for whatever reasons, studied Japanese culture and language with sympathy and perception; or from the Englishman Will Adams (1564–1620), adviser to the Shogun Ieyasu; and Richard Cocks (1566–1624), the incompetent British East India Company director in Hirado, whose lively diary shows an observant and keen interest in the Japanese scene. After the banishment of the Catholics by a Japanese Government terrified of their powerful secular connections with European colonialists, their detailed Latin descriptions of the far-distant islands became all but forgotten, except in Rome. For the next two centuries sporadic accounts of Japan were produced in spite of rather than because of the Dutch connection. The land which was about to produce the art of *Ukiyoe* had, indeed, become unknown.

The Dutch East India Company ships brought back to Europe very occasional examples of graphic art, acquired by the few among their employees who over those two centuries took an interest in Japanese culture. The first was Englebert Kaempfer (1651–1710), a German physician masquerading as Dutch to Japanese officials at Nagasaki, who were far too isolated to tell north Europeans apart from each other. (It is a curiosity of history that of the four Company men mentioned here who did take a real interest in Japan only one was actually Dutch.)

Kaempfer was in Nagasaki from 1690 to 1692, and on his return wrote his extensive, informative but only partly perceptive *History of Japan* (first published, as it happens, in English, in 1727). He brought back to Germany some woodblock illustrated books, now in the collection of the British Library, similar in type to nos 3 and 5 in this book. They were indeed among the earliest form of printed *Ukiyoe*. Typically for the time, they were of interest only to a scholarly few, among whom was Sir Hans Sloane (1660–1753), who bought them and other Japanese antiquities from Kaempfer's widow. Sloane's was the founding collection of the British Museum.

The Swedish botanist Carl Thunberg (1743–1824) was in Nagasaki in 1775. Apart from his work on Japanese flora, he brought back some coloured woodblock prints which are still preserved in the Ethnographical Museum in Stockholm, the earliest Japanese sheet prints surviving anywhere with a firmly documented date. They included works by Harunobu and Koryūsai, then the most fashionable and up to date of *Ukiyoe* artists in Japan itself (see nos 50–8, 66–73); but there is no evidence that they were seen in Europe as more than curiosities, or even noticed at all.

The lone Dutchman to study Japan's culture with enthusiasm was Isaac Titsingh (?1744–1812). On his return from his three tours of duty in Nagasaki he wrote and lectured extensively in Europe, including England, and his writings helped keep some knowledge of Japan alive among European intellectuals when the traditional exports of porcelain and lacquer had virtually ceased. A number of his manuscripts are still in the British Library. He is known to have brought back both antiquities and prints to Europe, although they became dispersed among collectors and scholars. It was quite possibly through him that the botanist and explorer Sir Joseph Banks (1743–1820) acquired his copy of Utamaro's *Ehon Mushi Erabi* (the 'Insect Book'), published in 1788. This was the second known example of Japanese pictorial art, after Kaempfer's, to enter the British Museum's collections, when it was bequeathed with Banks's library after his librarian's death. The example illustrated here (book 20) is, however, a copy in an even finer state from the Hillier Collection. There is no evidence that this great and beautiful example of woodblock printing was regarded in Britain at the time as anything more than a botanical source-book; plants are far more evident in it than the insects of the title.

It is one of those tantalising might-have-beens of history to wonder what would have followed had Sir Stanford Raffles (1781–1826) succeeded, when Lieutenant-Governor of Java, in taking over the Dutch monopoly in Japan on the grounds that they were Napoleon's allies. But he was outwitted by the Dutch Chief Merchant (*Operhoofd*) who stuck to his post until the Napoleonic Wars were over. In spite of his interest in Japanese culture, Raffles apparently brought back no examples of pictorial art. Meanwhile the European monopoly of access to the distant islands remained with the Dutch until 1853.

It was in fact another German doctor, again working for the Dutch East India Company, who was to bring back the first really comprehensive group of Japanese cultural material to the West. This was Philipp Franz von Siebold (1796–1866),

expelled from Japan in 1829, after a six-year stay, on the suspicion that he was a spy. Most of his extensive collections of artefacts and art were bought by the Dutch Government and formed the basis of the National Museum of Ethnography in Leyden. They included over 2,000 *Ukiyoe* prints in albums and portfolios, many of which were used as the basis for illustrations for Siebold's great work on Japan, *Nippon* (1832–58). Yet those illustrations were so thoroughly transformed by the Western engravers that they can have given no impression of the true flavour of Japanese art, whether of *Ukiyoe* or any other school. Nevertheless, just a few of the illustrations are fairly accurate copies of woodblock prints in outline – from original Japanese books – and must have been among the first hints of *Ukiyoe* style to have come to the notice of the European public. The originals seem to have been consulted hardly at all, as many of them were unpacked virtually for the first time in preparation for their publication in 1975.

The greater number of the Siebold prints were new or recent at the period of his Japanese residence and are dominated by the now familiar figures of Hokusai, Hiroshige, Eizan, Eisen and Kunisada, yet there were earlier artists represented, including Okumura Masanobu, Harunobu, Kiyonaga, Shunshō, Sharaku and Utamaro, suggesting that works by these celebrated *Ukiyoe* print designers were still available in Nagasaki or Edo. To the latter city Siebold went in 1826 on a diplomatic visit. His rather noticeable lack of diplomacy may have contributed to his expulsion three years later, although he was allowed to return much later in his life after the ending of the Seclusion policy. Some of his prints were first displayed in 1845, but again they seem to have made no impression.

It is tempting to speculate whether Siebold was the source of the woodblock book *Raikin Zui* (book 31) published in 1789, which has a British Library date-stamp for 1863 and was later transferred to the sub-Department of Oriental Prints and Drawings in the British Museum. It is one of the glories of Japanese woodblock printing, but like the 'Insect Book' it was probably acquired as a curiosity rather than a work of art. Ironically, it is now one of only two copies in existence, the other being in Ireland. In truth, like the 'Insect Book', it is not really *Ukiyoe* in style at all. As the above accounts suggest, the West was not yet ready for the art of the Floating World.

This was all to change very quickly indeed with Perry's expeditions and the opening of Japan. In 1858 diplomatic agreements were made also with France, Russia and Britain, and educated Europeans began to visit the country in large numbers. Books about Japan began to appear, including Sir Rutherford Alcock's *The Capital of the Tycoon* (1863). This was the first to discuss Japanese art, including prints, at moderate length in English. His collection of prints formed part of the Japanese section of the International Exhibition in London in 1862, and a year later the artist Frederick Leighton gave a lecture to the Fine Arts Society on Japanese art. It was published in fifty copies, each with an original *Ukiyoe* point as an insert. In those days, as the Japanese themselves lost faith in *Ukiyoe* under the impact of Westernisation and modernisation, so did the prints flood into the hands of enthusiastic Western aesthetes and collectors already disillusioned with that same technological world.

In France the enthusiasm became a mania which gave birth to the term *Japonisme*. It had begun as early as 1856 with the often-told story of the discovery by Bracquemond of Hokusai's printed *Manga* miscellanies at the workshop of his printer. In the 1870s and 80s no artist and few writers could afford to ignore the near obsession with things Japanese, of which *Ukiyoe* prints were the most easily available. James McNeill Whistler, who returned to London from Paris in 1859, remained closely in touch with France and was important in fostering the fascination with the Japanese print in Britain.

The collecting of *Ukiyoe* prints in the British Museum began very half-heartedly in 1860, with some relatively minor and recent Utagawa works acquired, it seems, merely as representations of the type, and hardly progressed for another generation. However, the acquisition in 1881 of the collection of Japanese and Chinese paintings formed by William Anderson added some 300 items claimed to be of the *Ukiyoe* School, and a handful of which were,

including Hokusai's splendid painting of Tametomo (no. 166). This event provided an impetus to begin in 1902 the serious building up of the collection by the curator, art historian and poet, Laurence Binyon (1869–1943). As a member of the then relatively intimate London intellectual and artistic world, he knew most of the major collectors, who were in their turn the heirs of the *Japonisme* craze of a generation earlier. Binyon was able to buy, beg or receive by bequest many of these collections, including those of Sir Ernest Satow, Arthur Morrison (prints and paintings) and Oscar Raphael. With the setting up in 1912 of a special sub-Department of Oriental Prints and Drawings, Binyon was able to take over many of the finest illustrated books, until then held as reference material in the Department of Oriental Printed Books (now part of the British Library). From then on the *Ukiyoe* collection grew consistently until the mid-1960s, and by then had reached its present richness. After that a combination of Western, especially American, enthusiasm for the *Ukiyoe* print, and a growing respect in Japan itself for this once-despised popular art led to the great and continuing rises in prices which now reflect the worldwide regard for the art of the Floating World.

The most recent major addition to the British Museum's holdings of *Ukiyoe* was the Jack Hillier collection of over 600 woodblock-printed books and albums of all schools, acquired in 1979. Until then Japanese connoisseurs had not paid the same respect to books as to sheet prints or paintings. The result was that Hillier was able to build up a collection of examples in an extremely fine state, including a large number of the *kyōka* album masterpieces published by Tsutaya Jūsaburō. All the books and albums illustrated here, bar eight, are from his collection.

GLOSSARY

abunae   'Risqué pictures' popular in the mid-eighteenth century, more revealing of the body than was normally the case.

bakufu   The military government, dominated in the period 1600–1868 by the Tokugawa family.

benie   'Pink picture'. Hand-coloured woodblock prints employing a pink pigment derived from the safflower (*benibana*); popular *c*.1720–40.

benigiraie   'Red-hating picture'. Paintings or prints with a muted colour scheme, particularly popular in the 1780s and 90s.

benizurie   Woodblock prints with two printed colours, generally pink and green; popular *c*.1740–55.

bijinga   Paintings or prints of beautiful women.

bikuni   Also *utabikuni*. Nuns who travelled the countryside preaching to audiences of common people.

bugaku   An ancient form of court dancing which originated in continental Asia.

Bunraku   Puppet theatre with chanted accompaniment.

chōnin   'Townsmen'. Merchants and artisans living in the cities who were not of the warrior class.

chūban   Medium size (slightly taller than wide) of woodblock print.

Chūshingura   'The storehouse of Loyal Retainers'. A samurai vendetta of 1703 which became the subject of countless puppet and Kabuki plays.

daimyō   'Great lords'. The warrior aristocracy of feudal Japan.

Edo (Tokyo)   Headquarters of the Shogunal government of the Tokugawa family from 1603 and the largest city in Japan by 1700. The period 1603–1868 is known as the Edo period.

egoyomi   'Picture calendar' in which the numbers for the long and short months of the lunar calendar were often ingeniously hidden.

fūkeiga   Paintings or prints of landscapes.

. . . ga   Painted/drawn by . . .

Genji Monogatari   A novel of courtly romance written by Lady Murasaki around the year AD 1000. Scenes from the fifty-four chapters were a common theme in later literature and art.

Gion   An entertainment district in Kyoto.

go   A board game like chequers.

haiku   Seventeen-syllable poem, often with themes from nature, always with a reference to the seasons.

hanshitae   Final preparatory drawing for a woodblock print.

hashirae   'Pillar picture'. Very tall narrow size of woodblock print, said to have been hung on wooden pillars.

. . . hitsu   From the brush of . . .

hosoban   Small, narrow, vertical size of woodblock print.

Ise Monogatari   A collection of courtly love tales centring on the character of Ariwara no Narihira, probably written in the eleventh century.

ishizurie   'Stone-printed picture'. A woodblock print employing white lines on a black background in imitation of stone rubbings.

jōruri   General term for ballad singing accompanied by the three-stringed *samisen*, especially used in the Bunraku theatre.

Kabuki   Popular theatre which began in the early seventeenth century.

kachōga   Paintings or prints of bird and flower subjects.

kago   A palanquin or sedan chair carried suspended from a pole by two bearers.

kai-awase   'Shell matching'. A courtly game involving matching two halves of clam shells, or poems and paintings drawn inside them.

kakemonoe   Very large, vertical size of woodblock print in imitation of a hanging-scroll painting.

Kamakura   Coastal city about fifty kilometres south-west of Edo (Tokyo) and seat of the first Shogunal (warrior) government from 1185 to 1333.

Kanō	The school of hereditary painters-in-attendance to the military government.	*Osaka*	Largest city in Western Japan, prominent as a business and financial centre.
kaomise	'Face showing'. The opening of the new Kabuki theatrical season held each year during the Eleventh Month (in Edo).	*Rokkasen*	'Six Poetic Immortals'. Famous poets of the courtly Heian period.
		saké	Rice wine.
kappazuri	'Stencil print', in which the outline is printed from a wooden block and the colours applied using stencils.	*sambasō*	An auspicious dance sequence performed at Kabuki theatres and at the New Year.
karakuri	Mechanical toy or other device.	*samisen (shamisen)*	Three-stringed 'banjo' widely played by popular entertainers of all kinds.
kimono	Long garment with flowing sleeves worn by both men and women.	*samurai*	Warrior class, representing the top ten per cent of society in feudal Japan.
Kisokaidō	A highway through the mountains from Edo to Kyoto with sixty-nine post stations along the route.	*sennin*	'Immortal' or 'hermit'. Often characters from Chinese Daoist legends.
koban	Small size of woodblock print.	*senryū*	Seventeen-syllable humorous or satirical verse.
kokyū	A small stringed instrument balanced upright on the knee and played with a bow.	*. . . sha*	Painted/copied by . . .
		Shichifukujin	Seven popular gods of good fortune.
koto	A courtly musical instrument with thirteen strings, each with its own ivory bridge, stretched across a long wooden sound-box. It lies in front of the player on the floor and is plucked with the fingers.	*shishi*	Mythical Chinese lion-like creature.
		Shogun	(Hereditary) head of the military government and *de facto* ruler of Japan. From 1600 to 1868 always a member of the Tokugawa family.
kyōka	'Crazy verse'. Thirty-one-syllable comic verse, often in parody of classical poetry.	*shōjō*	Mythical sprite-like creature fond of saké.
		shosa(goto)	Dance interlude in Kabuki theatre.
Kyoto	Ancient capital of Japan from AD 794 to 1868. The Imperial family and court nobility continued to reside there until 1868.	*sugoroku*	A board-game akin to backgammon.
		Sumiyoshi	A school of painting that was an offshoot of the courtly Tosa style, later patronised by the military government in Edo (Tokyo).
mitate	Parody or reworking of a classical theme in later theatre, literature or art.		
mizue	'Water picture'. A kind of full colour woodblock print that had a coloured instead of black outline, which enjoyed a brief vogue in the 1760s.	*sumizurie*	An uncoloured woodblock print in *sumi* ink.
		Sumō	Wrestling.
		surimono	*De luxe*, small edition woodblock prints often commissioned by poetry clubs or as invitations.
nagauta	'Long song'. Ballad singing with *samisen* accompaniment, particularly associated with the Kabuki theatre.	*Takarabune*	Lucky treasure ship which, according to legend, brings wealth at the New Year.
nishikie	'Brocade picture'. Full colour woodblock prints, first perfected in Edo in 1764/1765.	*Tanabata*	The Star Festival on the Seventh Day of the Seventh Month.
Niwaka	Festival in the Yoshiwara pleasure quarter in the Eighth Month.	*tane*	A woodblock print hand-coloured with red lead (*tan*) pigment.
Nō	The classical theatre of Japan, patronised mainly by the aristocracy.	*tanzaku*	Small narrow slip of paper on to which poems are written.
ōban	The most common, large size of woodblock print.	*tengu*	A mythical creature with wings and a beak but the body of a man.
obi	Decorative sash worn with a kimono.	*Tōkaidō*	A highway along the coast from Edo
ōōban	Extra large size of woodblock print.		

	to Kyoto with fifty-three post stations along the route.
tsuitate	A free-standing room-divider, often decorated with paintings.
uchikake	Long garment worn by women over their kimono.
uchiwae	Oval-shaped woodblock print intended to decorate a non-folding fan (*uchiwa*).
ukie	'Floating pictures'. Prints and paintings showing the influence of Western 'vanishing-point' perspective.
Ukiyoe	'Picture of the floating world'. Also the name given to the popular school of painters and woodblock print artists working in Japanese cities in the seventeenth, eighteenth and nineteenth centuries.
ukiyo-zōshi	'Novel of the Floating World'. Novels of urban life, frequently erotic, common in the late seventeenth and early eighteenth centuries.
urushie	'Lacquer picture'. A type of hand-coloured woodblock print which imitated the appearance of black lacquer by applying glue to areas printed in black ink; popular *c*.1720–40.
wakashū	Young man, sometimes effeminate.
yakushae	Paintings or prints of Kabuki actors.
Yamatoe	Native style of painting with simple outline and flat colour.
Yokohamae	Prints depicting the foreigners in Edo after 1853.
Yoshiwara	The main Pleasure Quarter in Edo (Tokyo) licensed by the military government. Called Shin (New) Yoshiwara after 1657.

BIOGRAPHIES OF ARTISTS

Chōyōdō ANCHI
Worked *c*.1711–36
Art names: Chōyōdō, Anchi

Paintings of beauties, and about ten large vertical prints of standing beauties by Anchi are known. Particularly talented among Kaigetsudō Ando's pupils, he alone was permitted to use the 'An' character of his teacher's name. Some of his paintings include the art name Chōyōdō in the signature; but all the prints are signed 'Drawn for pleasure by the Japanese artist Anchi, of the Kaigetsudō line' and sealed 'Anchi'. Almost all the prints were published by Maruya.

Ippitsusai BUNCHŌ
Worked *c*.1756–1801, but full colour prints limited to *c*.1767–73
Artistic training: Pupil of Ishikawa Yukimoto

Bunchō developed a more realistic style of actor portraiture, together with Katsukawa Shunshō, and produced many works in *hosoban* format. He had a very singular approach to his subjects: his figures are very slender but described with rounded, swelling lines that give them a sure sense of volume. His unusual talent for bringing out the role portrayed by means of very small variations in the actor's expression or deportment produced a very idiosyncratic personal style.

Hanegawa CHINCHŌ *c*.1679–1759
Worked *c*.1711–36
Artistic training: Pupil of Torii Kiyonobu I
Art names: Chinchō, Motonobu, Okinobu, Ejōsai, Sandō

An artist from the period of *tane* and *benie* prints, Chinchō is known more as an illustrator of cheap novels than a designer of single-sheet prints. His wide-ranging activities included actor critiques and guides to the Yoshiwara pleasure quarter. Chinchō was a major illustrator of the period, together with the Torii School artists, Okumura Masanobu and Kondō Kiyoharu.

Eishōsai CHŌKI
Worked late 1700s–early 1800s
Art names: At first, Chōki; changing to Shikō *c*.1795–6; reverting to Chōki in 1801. Also Eishōsai, Hyakusen

Chōki designed prints of women during the 1790s and early 1800s. He evolved a soft, intimate manner of depicting beauties which was highly individualistic in character. He also designed actor portraits in the manner of Sharaku and book illustrations.

Keisai EISEN 1791–1848
Worked c.1817–47
Artistic training: Pupil of Kanō Hakkeisai, Kikugawa Eiji and
    Kikugawa Eizan
Art names: Eisen, Keisai, Kokushunrō
Noms de plume: Ippitsuan Kakō, Mumeiō, etc.
Family name: Ikeda; common name: Zenjirō

A designer of prints of women of the late Edo period,
Eisen in the 1820s produced lurid bust portraits of women
of cloying sensuality, which rival the work of Kunisada.
His style is regarded today as the height of 'decadent'
beauty. He also gave a new flavour to landscape prints by
introducing elements of Kanō style to produce a more
modern sense of design.

Hosoda EISHI 1756–1829
Worked c.1786–1829
Artistic training: Pupil of Kanō Eisen'in Michinobu. Also said to
    have studied with Bunryūsai
Art name: Chōbunsai
Name: Tokitomi; common names: Taminosuke, Yasuburō

One of the leading painters of women of the 1790s, Eishi
was a vassal of the Shogunate with a generous stipend of
500 *koku* (90,000 litres) of rice. He drew elegant, refined,
idealised portraits of women based on the style of
Kiyonaga, establishing his own school and serving as a
rival to Utamaro. In the late 1790s he ceased to design
woodblock prints and concentrated exclusively on
paintings, at his own leisure.

Chōkōsai EISHŌ
Worked 1793–9
Artistic training: Pupil of Hosoda Eishi
Art names: Eishō, Chōkōsai, Shōeidō

The most prolific artist of prints of women among Eishi's
pupils, Eishō's forte was bust portraits of courtesans, and
in comparison with Eishi his women are homely and
sweet. The majority of Eishō's prints were issued by the
publisher Yamaguchiya Chūsuke.

Ichirakutei EISUI
Worked 1797–1804
Artistic training: Pupil of Hosoda Eishi

Among Eishi's pupils, Eisui was the third most prolific
after Eishō and Eiri in terms of the number of his colour
prints. His speciality was bust portraits derived from the
late 1790s' works of Utamaro, and there is a particularly
fine group in which the face of each courtesan completely
fills the sheet. Eisui also provided illustrations for the
popular novels of Jippensha Ikku.

Kikugawa EIZAN 1787–1867
Worked c.1804–67
Artistic training: Studied with his father Eiji and also with Suzuki
    Nanrei
Art names: Eizan, Chōkyūsai, Jigyokuya
Family name: Kikugawa; common name: Mangorō

Eizan produced many prints of women c.1805–20, adding
a quiet refinement to the late style of Utamaro. He was the
principal designer of prints of women of this period.

Yamamoto FUJINOBU
Worked 1751–72

Fujinobu produced prints of beauties in Harunobu style
and actor prints.

Yashima GAKUTEI c.1786–1868
Worked c.1814–67
Artistic training: First a pupil of Tsutsumi Tōrin III; later of Hokkei
Art names: Gakutei, Ichirō, Gogaku, etc.
Name: Harunobu, later Sadaoka

Gakutei mainly designed *kyōka surimono* and illustrated
kyōka anthologies. He also wrote his own comic fiction.

Seigyū GYŌCHIN
Worked c.1751–64
Art names: Seigyū, Seigyūsai, Tekidō, Suiseki, Suisekidō, Gyōchin

Gyōchin is known for several paintings of beautiful
women, and pillar prints.

Yoshida HAMBEI
Worked c.1664–89
Artistic training: Said to have studied the style of the artist Shōgorō

A Kyoto artist of the early period of *Ukiyoe*, Hambei was
the equivalent of Hishikawa Moronobu in Edo. Although
few of his works are signed, he is thought to have been
active in many areas of book illustration: popular novels,
jōruri books, accounts of famous places, etc. There are sets
of erotic prints which have also been attributed to him.

Suzuki HARUNOBU 1724–70
Worked 1760–70
Artistic training: Unclear, but there are theories that he was a pupil
    of either Nishimura Shigenaga or Nishikawa Sukenobu
Art names: Shikojin, Chōeiken

The leading artist of prints of beautiful women in the
1760s, Harunobu originally based his style on that of
Nishikawa Sukenobu but gradually became more
individual. He participated as an artist in the parties to
exchange calendar prints in 1765 and 1766, and became the
most important designer of prints of beauties as a result of
his major contribution to the establishment of the full
colour *nishikie* print. He was a prolific artist of *chūban* prints
showing the manners and customs of women, and
completely dominated his generation, giving rise to many

imitators. The special qualities of Harunobu's prints are their lyricism and purity of feeling; he invites the viewer into a special, dreamlike world.

Utagawa HIROSHIGE 1797–1858
Worked c.1817–58
Artistic training: Pupil of Utagawa Toyohiro; also studied with
  Okajima Rinsai and Ōoka Umpō
Art names: Hiroshige, Ichiyūsai, Ichiryūsai, Ryūsai, Utashige
Family name: Andō; common name: Tokubei

The leading landscape artist of the *Ukiyoe* school, Hiroshige was the son of an official in the fire department. In the 1820s he was active in many areas: actor prints, warrior prints, prints of women, etc. He started producing landscape prints in the early 1830s, establishing his own unique style with the series 'Famous Places in Edo' (Ichiyūsai signature) and 'Fifty-three Stations of the Tōkaidō Highway' of 1832–3. He continued to excel at views of famous places throughout his career and managed to express in great detail the poetic sensibility inherent in the climate and topography of Japan and the people who lived there. Hiroshige also designed many masterpieces in the genre of bird and flower prints, once again creating a world where poetry and painting combined.

Totoya HOKKEI 1780–1850
Worked c.1800–48
Artistic training: Pupil of Kanō Yōsen'in Korenobu; later of
  Katsushika Hokusai
Art names: Hokkei, Aoigaoka, Kyōsai, Kien, Go Hokkei

A senior pupil of Hokusai, Hokkei mostly produced *surimono* or illustrations to *kyōka* anthologies.

Katsushika HOKUSAI 1760–1849
Worked 1779–1849
Artistic training: Pupil of Katsukawa Shunshō; also said to have
  studied with Kanō Yūsen, Tsutsumi Tōrin III, Sumiyoshi
  Hiroyuki and others
Art names: Shunrō (to c.1794), Sōri (1794–8), Hokusai (1797–1819),
  Taitō (1811–20), Iitsu (1820–34), Manji (1834–49), etc. Used more
  than thirty other art names, such as Gakyōjin
Family name: Nakajima; common name: Tetsuzō

The leading *Ukiyoe* artist of the later Edo period, Hokusai had the longest career of any of them – more than seventy years – and during this time changed his style many times, making unique contributions in all fields. As his art name 'Gakyōjin' suggests, he was indeed 'mad with painting'. Particularly fine are the paintings and *surimono* from his Sōri period onwards; the *kyōka* anthologies, illustrated books and Western-style prints of his Hokusai period; the illustrated books and painting manuals of his Taitō period onwards; the series 'Thirty-six Views of Mount Fuji' of his Iitsu period.

Sugimura JIHEI
Worked 1680–1704
Art names: Jishin, Masataka

Sugimura Jihei was the nephew of Sugimura Kudayū, who was also the adoptive father of Sugimura Kihei, one of the famous forty-seven samurai involved in the Chūshingura vendetta. An important artist of the formative period of *Ukiyoe*, to be ranked with Hishikawa Moronobu, he produced single-sheet prints on *jōruri* or genre themes, sets of erotic prints, erotic books, illustrated books and illustrated popular novels. Many of his works are imbued with a wonderful sense of vivacity, and his female figures, done purely in black and white, are drawn with an undulating, rounded line. Almost no paintings by him are known.

Kondō KIYOHARU
Worked 1704–36
Common name: Sukegorō

An important artist of book illustrations in the generation following Moronobu, Kiyoharu's wide range of activities included illustrations for popular novels, actor critiques and guides to the Yoshiwara pleasure quarter; also many single-sheet prints, maps and broadsheets. He devised a popular new style for illustrated anthologies of *kyōka* poems, beginning with *Dōke hyakunin isshu*. He was also active as a painter.

Torii KIYOHIRO
Worked 1751–64
Artistic training: Torii School

One of the leading artists of the era of two-colour *benizurie* prints, Kiyohiro's works are mainly concentrated into the period 1751–8, and the majority were published by Maruya Kohei. He designed prints of both actors and beauties but particularly excelled in large *benizurie* prints of women. Although his style follows closely that of Ishikawa Toyonobu, Kiyohiro's prints are highly praised for their youthful vigour and power.

Torii KIYOMASU I
Worked 1704–22
Artistic training: Torii artist. Likely that he was the eldest son of
  Kiyonobu I

Together with Torii Kiyonobu I, Kiyomasu I was one of the principal artists of the first generation of the Torii School. A prolific artist whose work reached its peak c.1710–15, he developed the Kiyonobu I style still further into bold actor prints and polished, elegant designs of beautiful women. The end of his career remains obscure, but he is thought to have died at an early age, c.1720–5.

Torii KIYOMASU II (dates unknown; one theory suggests
    1706–64)
Worked 1724–64
Artistic training: Said to have been second-generation head of the
    Torii School

One of the principal artists of the Torii School during the
period of *benie* and *urushie* prints, together with Kiyonobu
II. Very active in many genres, his style is similar to
Kiyonobu II.

Torii KIYOMITSU 1735–85
Worked 1747–85
Artistic training: Third-generation head of the Torii School
Common name: Kamejirō

Said to be the second son of Kiyomasu II, Kiyomitsu was a
leading artist in *Ukiyoe* circles *c*.1760–5. In addition to
placards and playbills for Kabuki theatre, he also designed
many *hosoban* actor prints and illustrations for popular
novels. He faithfully followed the Torii style in works
which nevertheless lack strength and vigour. In the late
1760s his output decreased under pressure from the new,
more realistic actor portraits by Bunchō and Shunshō.

Torii KIYONAGA 1752–1815
Worked *c*.1769–1815
Artistic training: Pupil of Torii Kiyomitsu; fourth-generation head
    of the Torii School
Family name: Seki (or Sekiguchi); common name Shinsuke, later
    Ichibei

The leading designer of prints of beautiful women of the
1780s, Kiyonaga was the son of Shirokoya Ichibei, a
bookseller in the Honzaimoku-chō district of Edo. During
the late 1760s and 70s, while assimilating the styles of
many artists, he was gradually working towards a unique
personal idiom based on realism. In the 1780s he replaced
Koryūsai as the principal designer of prints of women. The
special characteristics of Kiyonaga's figure style are a tall
stature (the head only one-eighth of the total stature) and a
vital and wholesome appearance. He was skilled at
groupings of figures, and there are many masterpieces
among his multi-sheet compositions. Kiyonaga also made
innovations in the depiction of Kabuki performances,
producing a series of *ōban* prints showing both actors and
accompanying musicians on stage. Subsequent to
becoming the fourth-generation head of the Torii School
around 1787, he withdrew increasingly from the designing
of woodblock prints.

Kondō KIYONOBU
Worked 1711–16
Artistic training: Unknown, but probably related to Kondō
    Kiyoharu
Art name: Hikkaidō

Known for single-sheet prints of topical events and
illustrations for books, Kondō Kiyonobu's style is close to
that of Kondō Kiyoharu.

Torii KIYONOBU I 1664–1729
Worked *c*.1697–1729
Artistic training: Studied with his father Kiyomoto
Common name: Shōbei

The first-generation head of the Torii School, Kiyonobu I
assimilated the manner of Moronobu and Jihei and
developed his own style. He was adept at prints of both
actors and beauties, but his greatest achievement was to
establish the single-sheet actor print as a genre. He laid the
basis for the Torii School, creating a style suitable for large
theatrical placards, described as 'gourd (bulbous) legs and
worm line'.

Torii KIYONOBU II
Worked 1724–60
Artistic training: Torii School

Together with Kiyomasu II, Kiyonobu II was one of the
principal Torii artists of their generation. He designed
exclusively *hosoban* actor prints and parodies of actor
prints, following the style of Kiyonobu I, but in a more
tame and modest manner, without his dynamism or grace.

Torii KIYOSHIGE
Worked 1729–?64
Artistic training: Torii School

Kiyoshige mainly designed actor prints, but he also did
prints of beauties, warriors and illustrations to novels.
Paintings by him also survive, and he seems to have been
an important figure in the Torii School. Kiyoshige's works
have more depth and dynamism than those by Kiyonobu
II or Kiyomasu II.

Shiba KŌKAN (Suzuki HARUSHIGE) 1747–1818
Worked *c*.1764–1818
Artistic training: Kanō School, studied the *Ukiyoe* style of
    Harunobu and then became a pupil of Sō Shiseki. Also had links
    with Hiraga Gennai and Odano Naotake and became a fervent
    student of Western-style painting
Art names: Suzuki Harunobu, Suzuki Harushige, Shōtei, Kōkan,
    Shun, Kungaku, Shumparō, Fugen, Mugen, Tōgen, etc.

The main Western-style painter of the Edo period, in his
youth Kōkan produced *chūban* prints of women in
Harunobu style, signed either Harunobu or Harushige,
into which he introduced the novelty of backgrounds
incorporating vanishing-point perspective. He then
turned his attention to paintings of beautiful women.
From the late 1770s, however, Kōkan became interested in
Western-style painting and succeeded in producing the
first copperplate etchings in Japan in 1783. He then began
the study of oil painting and became a fully fledged
Western-style painter.

Isoda KORYŪSAI
Worked c.1766–88
Artistic training: Unknown; said to be a pupil of Nishimura
    Shigenaga. May also have studied under Harunobu
Art names: Haruhiro (early), Koryū, Koryūsai
Name: Masakatsu; common name: Shōbei

Said to be a *rōnin* (masterless samurai) from the Tsuchiya
household in Ogawa-machi, Edo, Koryūsai lived at
Ryōgoku Hirokoji Yagenbori. In the late 1760s he
produced Harunobu-style prints of beautiful women using
the name Koryūsai Haruhiro. After the death of
Harunobu, he became a major painter of women and
produced a very large number of colour prints during the
1770s. He was particularly skilled at pillar prints. From the
mid-1770s until c.1782 he worked on a series of over a
hundred *ōban* prints, the 'New Year Patterns for Young
Leaves'. Around 1781 he received the title 'Hokkyō' and
from about this time he came to specialise in paintings, of
which he produced many grand examples.

Ganjōsai KUNIHIRO
Worked 1816–35
Artistic training: Pupil of Utagawa Toyokuni?
Art names: Kunihiro, Ganjōsai, Kōnantei; used art surnames
    Takigawa and Utagawa

One of the most talented artists producing actor prints in
Osaka in the 1820s, Kunihiro was also known as
Temmanya Kunihiro. About seventy per cent of his prints
were issued by the publisher Temmanya Kihei, so it is
possible they were one and the same individual.

Utagawa KUNIMASA 1773–1810 (according to one theory)
Worked 1795–c.1808
Artistic training: Pupil of Utagawa Toyokuni
Art names: Kunimasa, Ichijusai
Common name: Jinsuke

The most senior of the pupils of Toyokuni, Kunimasa was
a native of Aizu. In 1795 and 96 he produced a series of
bust portraits of actors based on the style of his teacher,
but with a new and fresh character to them. He went on to
produce three-quarter-length and full-length portraits.
After c.1804 he almost ceased to work.

Utagawa KUNISADA (Utagawa TOYOKUNI III) 1786–1864
Worked 1807–64
Artistic training: Pupil of Utagawa Toyokuni; later Hanabusa Ikkei
Art names: Kunisada (to 1843), Toyokuni (from 1844), Gototei,
    Kōchōrō, etc.
Family name: Tsunoda; common name: Shōzō

The leading *Ukiyoe* artist of the late Edo period, Kunisada
was active for a long time as the central figure in the
Utagawa School. He is said to have produced the largest
number of works of any *Ukiyoe* artist. Particularly notable
are his stylish, oddly bewitching prints of women of the
1820s and 30s and the fresh, new style of his actor prints.

Utagawa KUNIYOSHI 1797–1861
Worked c.1814–60
Artistic training: Pupil of Utagawa Toyokuni
Art names: Kuniyoshi, Ichiyūsai, Chōōrō, etc.
Family name: Igusa; common name: Magosaburō

One of the three principal *Ukiyoe* artists of the late Edo
period, together with Kunisada (Toyokuni III) and
Hiroshige, Kuniyoshi is particularly noted for his warrior
prints and prints of bizarre and comic subjects. He also did
fine Western-style landscape prints during the 1830s and
early 40s. Kuniyoshi had an extremely fertile imagination
and produced a steady stream of novel innovations: he
served as a source of vital energy in the late *Ukiyoe* world.

Kawanabe KYŌSAI (GYŌSAI) 1831–89
Worked 1849–89
Artistic training: Pupil of Utagawa Kuniyoshi, later Maemura Tōwa
    and Kanō Tōhaku
Art names: Kyōsai, Gyōsai, Chikamaro, Shōshō, Nyokū (Jokū),
    Nobuyuki
Name: Tōiku

A natural genius working in a wide range of fields of both
Ukiyoe and more classical styles of painting, Kyōsai
produced many so-called 'crazy sketches' of a uniquely
individual kind. He combined technical mastery with
generous wit and a grandeur of conception. Many of his
paintings are particularly fine.

MANGETSUDŌ
Worked 1740s
Art names: Mangetsudō, Kōrin

Mangetsudō is known for *benizurie* prints in the style of
Okumura Masanobu. Many take the form of triptychs
with *haiku* poems written above the design.

Kitao MASANOBU 1761–1816
Worked c.1778–90
Artistic training: Pupil of Kitao Shigemasa
Art names: Masanobu, Rissai
Nom de plume: Santō Kyōden

A senior pupil of Shigemasa, Masanobu produced some
single-sheet prints, illustrated books, illustrated *kyōka*
anthologies and paintings, but the vast majority of his
works were illustrations for novelettes. His works of comic
fiction are generally highly intellectual and expository in
nature.

Okumura MASANOBU 1686–1764 (according to one theory)
Worked c.1700–64
Art names: Hōgetsudō, Tanchōsai, Bunkaku, Baiō, Shimmyō
Common name: Gempachi

A leading figure in the pre-*nishikie* (full colour print)
period, Masanobu established his own school, building on
the styles of Hishikawa Moronobu and Torii Kiyonobu. In
his early years he was also influenced by the illustrated
books of the Kyoto artist Nishikawa Sukenobu. He had a

very high opinion of his own talents and continued to study and foster new developments in *Ukiyoe* throughout his career. Perhaps because he was also the proprietor of a publishing house, the Okumuraya in Torishio-chō, he made many experiments with new formats and techniques for woodblock prints. In particular he may have originated pillar prints (*hashirae*) and perspective prints (*ukie*). His wide-ranging activities included prints of beauties, actors, birds and flowers, warriors, etc.; also many paintings and woodblock printed books. His prints of beauties in the *tane* technique are full and rounded, and have a quality of gentleness which eschews too much vigour.

Kitao MASAYOSHI 1764–1824
Worked 1780–1824
Artistic training: Pupil of Kitao Shigemasa, later Kanō Yōsen'in Korenobu
Art names: Masayoshi, Keisai
Family name: Akabane, later Kuwagata; name: Tsugusane; common name: Sanjirō

During his period of activity as an *Ukiyoe* artist, Kitao Masayoshi produced mainly novelette illustrations. After 1794, however, when he became painter in attendance to the Tsuyama fief, he switched mainly to paintings and printed albums. He produced many instructional manuals on how to paint in 'abbreviated style' (*ryakuga-shiki*).

Tanaka MASUNOBU
Worked 1740s
Art name: Sanseidō

Particularly known for several horizontal *ōban* perspective prints of the *urushie* period, Masunobu also designed actor prints, calendar prints and paintings of beautiful women. It is not clear if he is the same individual as the Masunobu of the *nishikie* period.

Tachibana MINKŌ
Worked 1760s–70s
Art names: Minkō, Gyokujuken

Originally an embroiderer working in metal foils, Minkō moved from Osaka to Edo. He is particularly famous for his illustrated book 'Various Classes of Artisans in Coloured Pictures', which further developed techniques of stencil printing. Calendar prints for 1765 and several book illustrations by him are known.

Hishikawa MORONOBU *c*.1618–94
Worked 1668–94
Artistic training: Mainly Tosa School, and is thought to have been self-taught in other styles
Art names: Moronobu, Yūchiku (late)
Common name: Kichibei

The leading artist in Edo (Tokyo) during the formative period of *Ukiyoe*, he is regarded as founder of the school. In the early 1680s Moronobu amalgamated various artistic currents into a new 'Hishikawa' style. His depiction of contemporary manners and customs in ample, elegant, refined line and colour was extremely popular. His *œuvre* consists of more than a hundred illustrated books; more than fifty erotic picture-books; and erotic broadsheets, scenes of famous places and illustrations to *jōruri* texts in sets. The large number of paintings by him in all formats – handscrolls, screens and hanging scrolls – also attests to his immense popularity.

Furuyama MOROSHIGE
Worked *c*.1678–98
Artistic training: Pupil of Hishikawa Moronobu
Common name: Tarobei

Moroshige first used the art surname Hishikawa and lived in Hasegawa-chō. He is known for his sets of erotic prints, illustrations for popular novels, erotic books and illustrated books of actors. His style is similar to that of Moronobu's later years, and though rather muted his figures are full and rounded in character. Paintings by him are also known, but as yet no signed single-sheet prints.

Utagawa SADAHIDE 1807–73
Worked 1826–73
Artistic training: Pupil of Utagawa Kunisada
Art names: Sadahide, Gyokuransai, Gountei, Gyokuō
Family name: Hashimoto; name: Kenjirō

A senior pupil of Kunisada, Sadahide produced many single-sheet prints and book illustrations; he particularly demonstrated his individuality in the last years of the Edo period in *Yokohamae* and detailed panoramas in which map-like elements were added to a bird's-eye view.

Toriyama SEKIEN 1712–88
Worked *c*.1751–88
Artistic training: Pupil of Kanō Gyokuen Chikanobu
Art names: Sekien, Sengetsudō, Reiryōdō, Gyokujuken, Gessō

An artist who trained in the Kanō School which dominated Edo painting at the time, Sekien had many links with the *Ukiyoe* School, such as producing designs for novels and illustrated books and portraits for use as votive panels. He did not produce any single-sheet prints, but among his pupils were many who became *Ukiyoe* artists, most noticeably Utamaro.

Juka SEKIJŌ
Worked 1789–1808
Art names: Sekijō, Juka Sekijō, Shichū Sanjin, etc.
Family name: Kajiyama; name: Shigeyoshi; common name: Gorōbei

A samurai from Yamagata, in addition to his activities as a writer of popular fiction Sekijō designed colour prints and book illustrations. His style is similar to that of Utamaro's later years.

Tōshūsai SHARAKU
Worked 5th Month of 1794–1st Month of 1795

The most famous artist of prints of actors of the whole *Ukiyoe* School, Sharaku made his shock début with a series of twenty-eight bust portraits, with shiny dark mica backgrounds, of actors starring in the plays performed at the three Kabuki theatres in Edo in the Fifth Month of 1794. After producing well over a hundred designs during the next nine months, he suddenly ceased to work after the First Month of 1795. At present a total of 144 designs are known, and these are customarily divided into four periods. The twenty-eight *ōban* prints of the first period capture with a penetrating eye both the personal character and style of the actor concerned, as well as the particular role he is playing. This is then exaggerated for expressive effect. Sharaku's works of this kind have earned a worldwide reputation as the ultimate in portraiture. In the second period, which is represented by thirty-eight full-length designs of actors, many works are still of high artistic merit. In the third and fourth periods, however, there is a dramatic drop in quality. All Sharaku's designs were published by Tsutaya Jūsaburō. There is much debate as to Sharaku's true identity, but as yet no single theory has been generally accepted.

Kitao SHIGEMASA 1739–1820
Worked *c*.1761–1820
Art names: Shigemasa, Karan, Kōsuisai, Suihō Itsujin, etc.
Common name: Kyūgorō

The eldest son of the bookseller Suharaya Saburobei of Kodemma-chō, 1-chōme, Shigemasa produced colour prints and paintings, but was principally active as a book illustrator, designing illustrations for over two hundred titles of mainly picture books, erotic books and novelettes. Among his colour prints those of the 1770s are particularly fine – grand, elegant and full of delicacy. He was the founder of the Kitao School.

Nishimura SHIGENAGA ?–1756
Worked *c*.1716–56
Art names: Eikadō, Senkadō Hyakuju

A major artist of the period from *benie* to *benizurie*, Shigenaga was active in many fields: actor prints; landscape series such as 'Eight Views of Kanazawa' and 'Eight Views of Lake Biwa'; classical themes; bird, flower and animal prints; historical prints; parody prints; perspective prints. However, he particularly excelled in prints of beautiful women, which have about them a warm amplitude.

Nishimura SHIGENOBU
Worked 1730–41
Artistic training: Pupil of Nishimura Shigenaga?

Shigenobu also used the name Nishimura Magosaburō, so Magosaburō may be his common name. So far over thirty works by him have been identified, mainly *hosoban* prints

of actors or beauties. This makes him the most prolific artist of the time after Masanobu, Toshinobu, Shigenaga, Kiyonobu II and Kiyomasu II. Stylistically he is close to Shigenaga, Masanobu and Toshinobu. There is a theory that Shigenobu was an early name used by Ishikawa Toyonobu, but present evidence is inconclusive. Nevertheless, the style of his prints in the late 1730s is certainly extremely close to works by Toyonobu.

Yanagawa SHIGENOBU 1787–1832
Worked *c*.1804–32
Artistic training: Pupil of Katsushika Hokusai
Art names: Yanagawa Shigenobu, Rinsai, Kinsai, Ushōsai
Family name: Suzuki; common name: Jūbei

More prolific as an artist of *surimono*, illustrated books and illustrations for novels than single-sheet prints or paintings, Shigenobu was very influential on *Ukiyoe* circles in the Osaka-Kyoto area during his stay in Osaka in 1822–3.

SHŌKŌSAI Hambei
Worked *c*. 1795–1809
Artistic training: Pupil of Ryūkōsai Jokei

An artist of actor prints in Ōsaka, in addition to single-sheet prints and paintings Shōkōsai produced a wide range of books connected with the theatre, such as illustrated books of actors, and also illustrated novels and librettos. He followed his teacher Ryūkōsai's style and popularised it. He is credited with being the first Osaka artist to design bust portraits of actors, albeit in the small, narrow *hosoban* format.

Tamagawa SHŪCHŌ
Worked 1789–1804
Artistic training: Pupil of Ippitsusai Bunchō

Known for prints of women, as well as the series 'Childrens' Games of the Four Seasons', 'A Mirror of Fashionable Toilette' and 'A Mirror of Fashionable Couplings', Shūchō also produced perspective prints and novelettes. Many works have about them a sense of calm repose similar to that of Chōki.

Kubo SHUMMAN 1757–1820
Worked *c*.1779–1818
Artistic training: Pupil of Katori Nahiko, later Kitao Shigemasa
Art names: Shumman, Shōsadō
Family name: Kubota (or Kubo); common name: Yasubei

From the mid-1780s into the 90s Shumman produced relaxed and elegant colour prints and paintings after the Kiyonaga manner. He was particularly adept at *benigiraie* ('red-hating pictures') in muted colour schemes. After the 1790s he ceased to design single-sheet prints, specialising entirely in *surimono* and paintings.

Katsukawa SHUNCHŌ
Worked: c.1780–1800
Artistic training: Pupil of Katsukawa Shunshō
Art names: Shunchō, Kichisadō, Shien, Tōshien, Chūrin, Yūshidō

Although a pupil of Shunshō, Shunchō consistently followed the Kiyonaga style of drawing beautiful women, producing many attractive, well-balanced compositions with descriptive background landscapes.

Katsukawa SHUN'EI 1762–1819
Worked 1778–1818
Artistic training: Pupil of Katsukawa Shunshō
Art names: Shun'ei, Kyūtokusai
Family name: Isoda; common name: Kyūjirō

Shun'ei assimilated and further developed the style of his teacher Shunshō, producing mainly actor prints. The leading artist of the Katsukawa School in the 1790s, his bright, light, free and easy style influenced many contemporaries, particularly Toyokuni.

Katsukawa SHUNKYOKU
Worked c.1775–95
Artistic training: Pupil of Katsukawa Shunshō

Known for his prints of actors, beautiful women and perspective views, Shunkyoku also designed illustrations for novelettes and theatre programmes from 1776 to 1785.

Katsukawa SHUNSHŌ 1726–92
Worked c.1764–92
Artistic training: Pupil of Miyagawa Shunsui, said to have also studied with Kō Sukoku
Art names: Shunshō, Kyokurōsei, Yūji, Ririn, Rokurokuan, Jūgasei

Together with Ippitsusai Bunchō, Shunshō made a vital contribution to the development of realistic portrayal of Kabuki actors. After Bunchō ceased to design prints in the early 1770s, Shunshō was left pre-eminent in the field, heading the Katsukawa School and providing the lead in all types of actor portrayal. His style is basically realistic, employing a flowing line and bright, precise colouring: he manages to draw out the individual strengths of actors and depict them in a grand manner, without exaggeration. In the 1780s Shunshō turned his talents to paintings of beautiful women and produced many glorious examples. As was written at the time, 'A painting by Shunshō is worth one thousand pieces of gold'.

Katsukawa SHUNTEI 1770–1820
Worked c.1797–1820
Artistic training: Pupil of Katsukawa Shun'ei
Art names: Shuntei, Shōkōsai, Ryūryūsai, Gibokuan, Kyūko, Suihō Itsujin
Family name: Yamaguchi; common name: Chōjūrō

In addition to prints of beauties, actors and warriors Shuntei is notable for his experimentation in Western-style landscapes and *surimono*. He also designed many illustrations for popular novels.

SŌRI

This is an art name used by Katsushika Hokusai from 1794 to 1798, when he passed it on to his pupil Hishikawa Sōji. There is controversy over whether certain works signed 'Sōri' should be attributed to Hokusai or Sōji.

SUIFUTEI
Worked 1780s

An artist known only by his picture-book of portraits of actors, *Suifutei Gigafu* ('An Album of Humorous Pictures by Suifutei'); under a gloss of humour Suifutei managed to capture the artistic temperament and style of each actor in a very penetrating manner. This was important in establishing one of the courses which the depiction of actors would take in the Osaka-Kyoto area.

Nishikawa SUKENOBU 1671–1750
Worked c.1700–50
Artistic training: Said to have studied with Kanō Einō and Tosa Mitsusuke
Art names: Jitokusō, Jitokusai, Bunkadō
Common name: Uemon

A Kyoto *Ukiyoe* artist, Sukenobu became a retainer of the aristocratic Saionji family and was granted the court title Sakyō. He was the leading painter of beautiful women in the Osaka-Kyoto area during the early period of *Ukiyoe*. He perfected a fresh, new style of depicting women in a refined and ample manner, based on realism, and established his own school. Sukenobu produced many paintings of women, and his illustrated books total more than a hundred titles. He had a tremendous influence on later artists in Edo, particularly Suzuki Harunobu.

Katsumura TERUNOBU
Worked c.1716–36
Artistic training: Unknown, but possibly linked to Katsukawa Terushige

A small group of *urushie hosoban* prints by Terunobu are known. Most of these were published by Igaya.

Utagawa TOYOHARU 1735–1814
Worked c.1764–1814
Artistic training: Pupil of Toriyama Sekien
Art names: Toyoharu, Ichiryūsai, Senryūsai, Shōjirō
Common name: Tajimaya Shōjirō, later Shin'emon

Toyoharu designed many perspective prints during the later 1760s and 70s, laying the foundations for the development of landscape prints. From the 1780s onwards he concentrated on paintings of the fashions and customs of beautiful women. He was the founder of the Utagawa School.

Utagawa TOYOHIRO 1773–1829
Worked *c.*1788–1829
Artistic training: Pupil of Utagawa Toyoharu
Art names: Toyohiro, Ichiryūsai
Family name: Okajima; common name: Tōjirō

Toyohiro became most active as an artist from the late
1790s, producing prints and paintings of beautiful women,
a small quantity of landscapes and *surimono*, and many
book illustrations. His paintings include some particularly
fine examples.

Utagawa TOYOKUNI 1769–1825
Worked *c.*1788–1824
Art names: Toyokuni, Ichiyōsai
Family name: Kurahashi; personal name: Kumakichi

The artist who led the Utagawa School, the most prolific
and influential school of the late Edo period, Toyokuni
rose to prominence in *Ukiyoe* circles with the success of his
'Portraits of Actors on Stage' series, issued from 1794
onwards. His elegantly flowing line and cheerful colour
schemes produced a lively and vivid sense of realism
which established the direction for subsequent
developments in actor portraiture. He was also adept at
paintings and prints of women, but increasingly in the
nineteenth century Toyokuni's work in both genres
became more coarse and stultified.

Okumura TOSHINOBU
Worked 1716–51
Artistic training: Pupil of Okumura Masanobu
Art names: Kakugetsudō, Bunzen

One of the major artists of the *benie/urushie* era of *Ukiyo*,
Toshinobu's style follows that of his teacher Masanobu,
but is more animated and has a soft fullness to it. His
drawing is very detailed and has a particular charm which
often excels Masanobu.

Ishikawa TOYONOBU 1711–85
Worked *c.*1741–81
Artistic training: Said to be a pupil of Nishimura Shigenaga
Art names: Tanshōdō, Shūha

A major artist of prints of beautiful women in the *benizurie*
period, Toyonobu was adopted into the family which ran
the Nukaya lodging house in Kodemma-chō, 3-chōme and
took the name Shichibei. He set a rich tone for the late
1740s and early 50s with his pure, elegant and gentle style,
and particularly excelled in hand-coloured wide pillar
prints and large *benizurie* in shades of pink and green.

Kitagawa UTAMARO 1753–1806
Worked 1775–1806
Artistic training: Pupil of Toriyama Sekien
Art names: First known as Kitagawa Toyoaki, changing to Utamaro
   *c.*1781
Family name: Kitagawa; common name: Yūsuke, also Ichitarō

The most celebrated artist of women of the whole *Ukiyoe*
school, Utamaro's work blossomed steadily during the
1780s as a result of his close association with the publisher
Tsutaya Jūsaburō. He strove hard to develop a fresh and
cool new depiction of women, and after a period during
the late 1780s and early 90s when he concentrated on
illustrated albums and sets of prints inscribed with *kyōka*
poems, he managed to establish his own unique style and
replace Kiyonaga as the premier designer of prints of
women. He excelled at sensuous depictions, at conveying
the sense of the glistening skin of the female body and
capturing the most delicate nuances of emotional states, in
a very different manner from Kiyonaga. Over-production
may have contributed to a gradual slackening and
coarsening of design sense from the late 1790s onwards,
and Utamaro would never recapture his earlier greatness.
He produced many illustrated books, erotic prints and
some fine paintings.

THE PRINTS

NOTE

All publishers recorded in these descriptions are Edo, unless otherwise stated. In some entries the publisher is unknown and no details are given.

Dates of artists are given with a wide band where exact dates are not known, in which case they are identified by the prefix 'worked'.

Early Prints

HISHIKAWA MORONOBU
Worked 1668–94

1 *Cherry-viewing parties*,
   from the series 'Flower-viewing in Ueno'

Published by Yamagataya Ichirōemon
c. 1680
Woodblock with hand-colouring, 266 × 409 mm
1945. 11-1.046

This is one of a set of twelve sheets; a complete set
is in the Museum of Fine Arts, Boston, where the
title is recorded on the first sheet. The set is also
known in Japan as 'Sightseeing in Edo'.

Ueno is the hilly district in the north of old Edo,
and is still a favourite place for cherry-viewing in
April. A samurai with two attendants and five
women, also with two attendants, are shown
passing each other. The servants carry picnic
boxes and equipment on poles.

Attributed to
HISHIKAWA MORONOBU

2 The reward scene
   from *The Tale of Ōeyama*

Published by Urokogataya Sanzaemon
c. 1680
Woodblock with hand-colouring, 274 × 365 mm
1919.10-14.02

This is the final sheet of a set of twelve recounting
the legend of the subjugation of the flesh-eating
demon called the Shūten Dōji by the hero
Yorimitsu. With his companions Yorimitsu made
the demon drunk, cut off his head, released his
female captives, and returned in triumph to
Kyoto, where he presented the head to the
Emperor. In this scene he is receiving his official
commendation. Ōeyama was the name of the
Shūten Dōji's mountain lair, which gave its name
to the story. The attribution to Moronobu is a
tentative one.

Attributed to
SUGIMURA JIHEI
Worked 1680–1704

3 *Tokiwa Gozen at Fushimi*

c. 1690
Woodblock with very slight hand-colouring, 560 × 305 mm
1968.10-14.2

The title *Fushimi Tokiwa* is also the name of a
dance. The noblewoman Tokiwa Gozen, mistress
of Yoshitomo, fled following his defeat in the Heiji
wars of the late twelfth century. She travelled
barefoot in the snow into the mountains with her
three children, the youngest of whom was to
become Japan's greatest hero, Minamoto no
Yoshitsune. She was sheltered overnight by an
old couple at Fushimi, who in this print are shown
top left below the title cartouche. This is one of the
favourite subjects of popular art in the Edo period.

4

HIRONOBU

4 *The Birth of the Buddha*

Dated in the first 'third' of the rabbit month, the seventh year of
    Empo = AD 1679
Woodblock with hand-colouring, 575 × 422 mm
1957.4-13.017

Legends concerning the birth of the Buddha and his
early days are shown together, including his sprinkling
with water by two dragons, and the 'Seven Steps' taken
immediately following his birth when he pointed to
heaven and declared his own greatness. The date is
printed with a different block, so the print itself may be
earlier, the date being changed each year to celebrate the
Buddha's birthday on the eighth day of the fourth
month. This is not strictly a *Ukiyoe* print at all. Its artist,
known from the seal as Hironobu, was probably a
member of the official Kanō School of painters, but he
clearly cannot be the Kanō Hironobu known to have
lived in the early eighteenth century.

CHŌYŌDŌ ANCHI
Worked *c.* 1711–36

5 *A courtesan of Edo*

Published by Maruya
c. 1710–20
Woodblock, 590 × 319 mm
1910.4–18.175

One of the highest-grade Edo courtesans is shown in a
typically bold costume of the period, the outer garment
decorated with ivy leaves, cherry blossom, fans and
tasselled braids. The very large prints of the studio
founded by Kaigetsudō Andō in the early years of the
eighteenth century are in fact rarer than the paintings on
which the prints were based. The signature reads
'picture for amusement by the Japanese artist, Anchi,
last descendant of Kaigetsu'. Both Chōyōdō and
Kaigetsudō are studio names rather than family names.
The seal reads Anchi, and the publisher's mark is in the
shape of an egg-plant.

HANEGAWA CHINCHŌ
c. 1679–1759

6 *A travelling nun*
    as Tokiwa Gozen at Fushimi

Published by Sagamiya Yōbei
c. 1684–8
Woodblock with hand-colouring and sprinkled metal dust,
    328 × 161 mm
1945.11-1.03

For the story of Tokiwa Gozen see the print by Sugimura
(no. 3). Here she is portrayed by one of the entertainers
(*utabikuni*), who wandered Japan at the period of this
print dressed as nuns. She is accompanied by two
apprentices representing Tokiwa's elder sons. The
subject is really the dance *Fushimi Tokiwa*. The signature
is 'From the brush of Hanegawa Chinchō Motonobu'.

5

6

Attributed to
TORII KIYONOBU I
1664–1729

7 *The actor Ogino Sawanojō as a woman travelling*
c. 1700–4
Woodblock with hand-colouring, 275 × 157 mm
1931.5-13.022

A typical female impersonator of the period, he wears a special scarf which he originated and was called the 'Sawanojō hat' after him. The actor's paulownia-leaf crest is shown top right and on his outer garment. The expansively patterned dress is characteristic of the flamboyant Genroku era (1688–1704). The print is unsigned, but the confident attribution makes it a rare example of the early style of Kiyonobu I.

TORII KIYONOBU I

8 *Actors imitating shōjō*
Published by Emiya Kichiemon
c. 1716–20
Woodblock with hand-colouring and applied metal dust,
205 × 281 mm
1910.4-18.177

The *shōjō* are popular and mythical monkey-like
creatures who are very fond of saké and are
symbols of celebration. In this New Year print two
actors of the day imitate them, a great saké jar
between them. One holds a ladle and rides on a
huge water-turtle; the other holds a giant
saké-cup. His kimono displays the mallet motif of
the popular god Daikoku. In the background are
cranes, and the trio of lucky plants – bamboo,
plum blossom and pine. All of these symbols are
associated with good luck, long life and the New
Year. The signature is 'The brush of Torii
Kiyonobu'.

Attributed to
TORII KIYONOBU I

9 *The popular gods Ebisu, Hotei and Daikoku in the Treasure Ship*
Published by Emiya Kichiemon
c. 1716–20
Woodblock with hand-colouring and applied metal dust,
207 × 280 mm
1910.4-18.176

This is a New Year print, showing the *Takarabune*
which in Japanese popular lore sails into port on
New Year's Day loaded with treasures and
symbols of good fortune. Here it is occupied by
the three favourites from the group known as the
Shichifukujin ('the Seven Lucky Gods'). They are
Ebisu, catching a *tai* fish, eaten at the New Year;
Hotei with his Chinese fan; and Daikoku with his
mallet, flanked by casks of saké. They are
accompanied by Chinese boys who betray the
continental origin of these gods. The characters on
the sail read 'Much Money'. A poem each side of
the sail reads in Japanese the same backwards or
forwards, 'How good is the sound of the ship
riding the waves awaking all from their proper
sleep of this long night'.

TORII KIYONOBU II

10 *The actor Segawa Kikunojō in the play Matsukaze*
Published by Murataya Jirōbei
c. 1733–8
Woodblock with hand-colouring, 'lacquer' (ink and glue),
   and metal dust, 318 × 154 mm
1954.4-10.04

Matsukaze, carrying her water-buckets, discovers that
her beloved Yukihira has left his exile by the coast at
Suma. He has hung his cloak on the pine-tree with a
letter vowing he will return. He never in fact does. The
story was originally found in a Nō drama and converted
to the popular Kabuki theatre. The print is signed 'The
brush of Torii Kiyonobu'.

TORII KIYONOBU II
Worked 1724–60

11 *The actors Ogino Sawanojō as Godai no*
   Saburō and Segawa Kikunojō as Ono no
   Omachi
Published by Maruya Kūzaemon
c. 1733–8
Woodblock with hand-colouring, 'lacquer' (ink and glue),
   and metal dust, 322 × 151 m.n
1940.6-1.01

The subject of this Kabuki play seems to be an adaptation
of a scene from the life of the ninth-century poetess Ono
no Komachi (the usual reading of her name). A rival
male poet accused her of plagiarism, which she refuted
by washing the book from which he was quoting to show
that he had recently added the incriminating text. The
print is signed 'The brush of Torii Kiyonobu'.

TORII KIYOMASU I
Worked 1704–22

12 *The actor Ichikawa Danjūrō II as Soga no Sukeroku*
Published by Igaya
1716
Woodblock, 422 × 291 mm
1906.12-20.17

The Kabuki scene 'Sukeroku' was acted at the
Nakamura-za theatre in the first month of 1716. The
second-generation Danjūrō achieved such fame in this
heroic role that it became the symbol of his family's skill.
In this scene he stands outside a tea-house in the
Yoshiwara, the brothel quarter of Edo (Tokyo), watched
by two courtesans. This is one of a series by Kiyomasu,
which shares the title cartouche in the top right corner.
The print is signed Torii Kiyomasu.

12

13

14

TORII KIYOMASU I

13 *The actors Ichikawa Danzō and Ōtani Hiro*
    in the play Kusazurihiki

Published by Sagamiya Yohei
1717
Woodblock with *tan* (red) applied by hand, 525 × 315 mm
1906.12-20.18

It is not certain which of two plays performed in 1717 this
is. The incident shows Danzō trying to hurl a boat into
the sea. Hiro crashes through the side to prevent him.
The violent, shorthand style is typical of the Torii School
of artists in their depiction of *aragoto* ('rough stuff')
theatre parts. Such prints were clearly theatrical
broadsheets rather than the actor portraits of the next
generation, and this has resulted in their rare survival.
The print is signed Torii Kiyonobu.

TORII KIYOMASU II
Worked 1724–64

14 *Night rain at Karasaki,*
    from 'Eight Views of Ōmi'

Published by Igaya
c. 1724–36
Woodblock with hand-colouring, 'lacquer' (ink and glue), and
    metal dust, 314 × 156 mm
1906.12-20.15

This is the second of a set of eight traditional views of
Lake Biwa (Ōmi) to the east of Kyoto. The views were in
turn based on an older Chinese set called 'Eight Views of
the Xiaoxiang Rivers'. This is probably the earliest
Ukiyoe-school set on this subject, and also one of the
earliest Japanese landscape prints. The scene shows
peasants near a small Shintō shrine. The poem refers to
the famous pine-tree on the promontory there at
Karasaki. The print is signed 'The brush of the artist
Torii Kiyonobu'.

TORII KIYOMASU II

15 *Summer*, from 'Peasants in the Four Seasons'
Published by Igaya
c. 1724–36
Woodblock with hand-colouring, 'lacquer' (ink and glue), and
    metal dust, 290 × 125 mm
1906.12-20.36

Women are planting the young rice. A man brings plants
in baskets, and a woman with a child brings
refreshments. Scenes of the countryside and of peasant
life are rare in the *Ukiyoe* print before the nineteenth
century. This copy is trimmed, but others retain the
artist's and publisher's names printed at the bottom.

TORII KIYOSHIGE
Worked 1729–?64

16 *The actor Ichikawa Ebizō II as an Immortal*
Published by Urokogataya Magobei
c. 1741–8
Woodblock, 683 × 157 mm
1965.6-12.05

The subject is unidentified, but the man is a *sennin*, or
Immortal, derived from Chinese Daoism. Knowledge of
Chinese matters had increased with the lifting of the ban
on most book imports in 1720. The print is signed 'The
artist Torii Kiyoshige'.

15

16

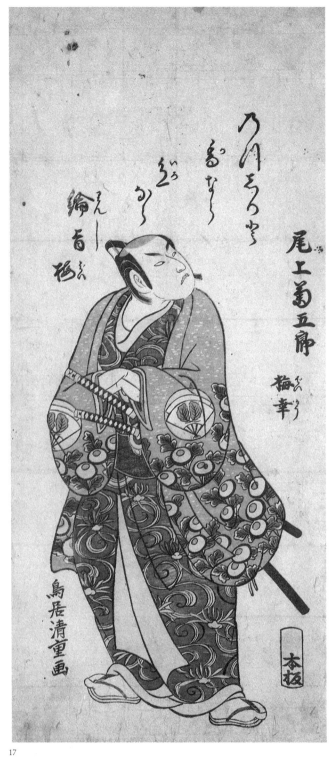

17

18

44

TORII KIYOSHIGE

17 *The actor Onoe Kikugorō I as a samurai*
Published by Maruya Kohei
c. 1751–64
Woodblock, 400 × 180 mm
1939.6-10.06

The Onoe family of actors specialised in military
and realistic parts. The poem is signed with the
actor's pen-name, 'Baikō'. The print is signed
'Painted by Torii Kiyoshige'.

TORII KIYOHIRO
Worked 1751–64

18 *The letter in the wind*

c. 1751–64
Woodblock, 432 × 310 mm
1945.11-1.06

A woman's paper handkerchiefs blow away, and
with them a love-letter she has been concealing.
Prints revealing parts of the female body not
usually seen were known as *abunae* ('dangerous
pictures') and were popular in the mid-eighteenth
century. The print is signed 'The brush of Torii
Kiyohiro'.

TORII KIYOHIRO

19 *The spinning top*
Published by Maruya Kohei
c. 1751–7
Woodblock, 294 × 136 mm
1907.5-31.4

A *wakashū* (young man of fashion) watches two
boys spinning a top. From the *senryū*
(light-hearted verse) inscribed above it is revealed
that the boys are brothers. The young man is
identified by the chequered pattern round his
collar as the actor Sanogawa Ichimatsu, then the
most popular actor of his time among women.
(The pattern came to be known as *Ichimatsu*.)
The papers hanging from the end of his sword
are assumed to be love-letters. The print is
signed 'The brush of Torii Kiyohiro'.

19

20

TORII KIYOHIRO

20 *The actors Yamashita Matatarō and*
Nakamura Tomijūrō
Published by Maruya Kohei
1755
Woodblock, 305 × 133 mm
1907.5-31.3

The print describes the transfer in November 1755 of the Kabuki actor Matatarō to the Nakamura-za theatre, where he joined Tomijūrō. The *haiku* poem inscribed on the print says that the scent of plum blossom (crest of Nakamura, in the role of a samurai, standing) has been added to the 'wheel of arrows' (the crest of Tomijūrō, in the role of a prostitute, kneeling and performing the Tea Ceremony). The print is signed 'The brush of Torii Kiyohiro'.

TORII KIYOHIRO

21 *Six actors under umbrellas*
Published by Maruya Shōbei
c. 1753–4
Woodblock, 289 × 449 mm
1910.4-18.178

This three-part composition was printed from three sets of blocks on to one piece of paper, and was probably intended to be cut up. The actors are shown under umbrellas, each bearing two identifying crests. From the right they are: Segawa Kikujirō, Arashi Wakano II, Nakamura Tomijūrō, Sanogawa Ichimatsu, Nakamura Kumetarō and Ichimura Kamezō. Tomijūrō's portrait is a travesty of the story where the ninth-century poetess Ono no Komachi prays for rain. Three *haiku* poems on the subject of rain are inscribed. The prints are each signed 'The brush of Torii Kiyohiro'.

KONDŌ KIYONOBU
Worked 1711–16

22 *Print of the procession of the companies of firemen*
Published by Komatsuya
Dated Shōtoku 4 = 1714
Woodblock with hand-colouring, 320 × 540 mm
1926.5-11.02

This print shows a procession of the Edo (Tokyo) fire service. The presence of a date and a censor's mark indicate that this was an official government commission, since such censorship did not become general until the 1790s. The fire service was set up in 1658 following a major Edo fire. The ten companies depicted in the top row are shown with their dates of foundation, districts, crests, stipends and other details. The print is signed 'The Japanese artist Kondō Kiyonobu'.

21

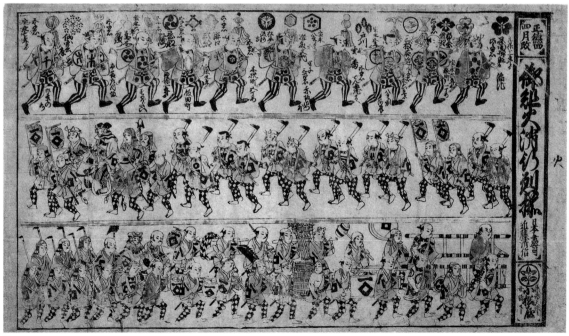

22

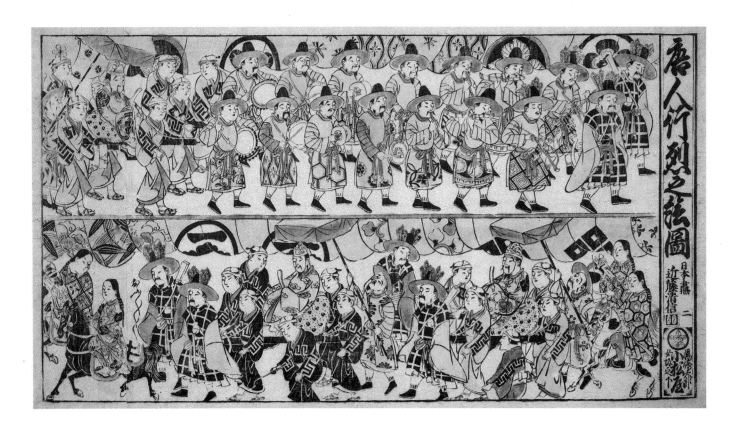

KONDŌ KIYONOBU

23 *Picture of the procession of the Chinese*
   (in fact, Koreans)

Published by Komatsuya
1711
Woodblock with hand-colouring, 325 × 555 mm
1924.7-14.05

This is the second of two sheets, which would
have butted together to form a continuous
composition. The scene depicts the Korean
embassy to the Shogun (military dictator) in Edo
(Tokyo) in 1711, and the character for 'Chinese'
used in the title seems to be a mistake. There were
in fact no Chinese embassies in the Edo period
(1603–1867), and the ordinary Japanese of the time
do not seem to have easily distinguished between
the two. Many of the Koreans are shown with the
tall hats and beards which so impressed the
Japanese of the period. The print is signed 'The
brush of the Japanese artist Kondō Kiyonobu'.

KONDŌ KIYOHARU
Worked 1704–36

24 *Evening Glow at Noshima,*
    from 'Eight Views of Kamakura'

Published by Tsuruya Kiemon
c. 1716–36
Woodblock with hand-colouring, 153 × 319 mm
1926.5-11.010

This is the fourth of a series which is otherwise
unknown, and which was based on the classical
Chinese set called 'Eight Views of the Xiaoxiang
Rivers'. Kamakura is an old town to the
south-west of Tokyo, and the nearby offshore
islands and Shintō shrines (one shown on the left)
were and are a tourist attraction. The print is
placed in a fan-shaped frame, and is signed 'The
brush of the craft-artist Kondō Kiyoharu'.

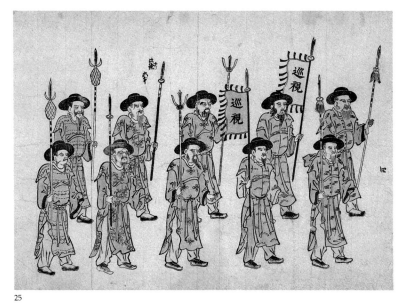

25

25

OKUMURA MASANOBU
?1686–1764

25 *The Korean embassy procession*
Published by Tsuruya Kiemon
1711
Woodblock with hand-colouring, 287 × 404 mm (each approx.)
1926.4-10.040 (1-10)

These are from a series of twelve, of which the first two
are missing from the British Museum's set. They were
probably intended to be made into a handscroll, in which
form they survive in other copies. The Korean embassy
of 1711 made a big impression, and these pictures of it
were printed on the orders of the military government.
The Japanese samurai accompanying the Koreans have
shaven heads and some carry swords. The missing first
sheet is signed 'Picture by the Eastern Japanese artist
Okumura Masanobu'. 'Eastern' refers to the city of Edo.
This is one of the earliest works of this major *Ukiyoe* artist
and publisher.

25

27

OKUMURA MASANOBU

26 *The actor Onoe Kikugorō I
playing the sasara*

Published by Hōgetsudō (one of Masanobu's imprints)
1741–8
Woodblock with hand-colouring, 657 × 228 mm
1928.7-18.02

The actor plays a woman with a traveller's hat. He
is holding a simple instrument made of split
bamboo which is played with a serrated bow. He
appears to be dressed to perform a sacred dance.
The print is signed 'The brush of Okumura
Bunkaku Masanobu', and there is an inscription
that it is a *true* production of the Hōgetsudō
publishing house, which had been the victim of
cheap copyists.

OKUMURA MASANOBU

27 *A scene from the play Dōjōji at the
Nakamura-za theatre*

Published by Okumuraya Genroku (one of Masanobu's
imprints)
1744
Woodblock with hand-colouring, 293 × 432 mm
1908.6-16.155

This is an *ukie* (perspective print) using the then
exotic European artistic convention of the
vanishing-point, although modified by Japanese
practice. It enabled Masanobu and others of the
time to depict crowded indoor scenes adequately.
This is a scene from a *jōruri* (drama with chanted
and musical accompaniment) called *Momochidori
Musume Dōjōji* ('The Dōjōji Play with a Hundred
Plover-maidens'). The heroine is entering left on
the raised walkway, while two comic priests are
seen on the main stage in front of the great bell
which features in the story. The print is signed in
other versions by Okumura Masanobu, but in this
version it has been half trimmed off.

28

OKUMURA MASANOBU

28 *A 'first night' at the Nakamura-za theatre*
Published by Okumuraya Genroku (one of Masanobu's imprints)
1745
Woodblock with hand-colouring, 438 × 650 mm
1910.6-14.02

This 'perspective print' shows in vivid detail the inside of one of Edo's greatest theatres, the audience relaxing, eating and drinking as still happens at traditional Kabuki performances. The actors' crests on the lanterns enable the print to be dated to 1745. One of the actors is named on the print as Ichikawa Ebizō, but the records do not agree that he appeared on this occasion; this composition may therefore be a generalised evocation of a Nakamura-za 'first night' (literally, 'face-showing' by an actor, occurring at the beginning of the season in the eleventh month). This copy is trimmed, but complete examples include the artist's and publisher's names in the margins.

OKUMURA MASANOBU

29 *The New Year's First Playing*
Published by Okumuraya Genroku (one of Masanobu's imprints)
1755
Woodblock, 423 × 307 mm
1910.6-14.1

Two geisha are seen with an attendant carrying a box for a musical instrument – probably the three-stringed *samisen* – which is to have its first playing of the New Year. One of the geisha is looking at the programme of the Nakamura-za Kabuki theatre for late 1755 and the New Year of 1756. The *senryū* (light-hearted poem) above comments that the women are more interested in the theatre than in their jobs. The print is signed 'Painted by Hōgetsudō Tanchōsai Okumura Bunkaku Masanobu'. Most Japanese artists had a variety of names, but they were rarely used in such close profusion as here.

OKUMURA TOSHINOBU
Worked 1716–51

30 *Types from Kyoto, Edo and Osaka*
Published by Izutsuya Chūzaemon
c. 1716–36
Woodblock with hand-colouring, 'lacquer' (ink and glue), and
   metal dust, 312 × 157 mm
1906.12-20.41

This composition shows types from the three great cities of Japan. In the centre is an Edo (Tokyo) townsman with his arm round a glamorous young man from Osaka. Behind sits a Kyoto prostitute in the tea-house at the front of a brothel. The print is signed 'The brush of the Japanese craft-artist Okumura Toshinobu'.

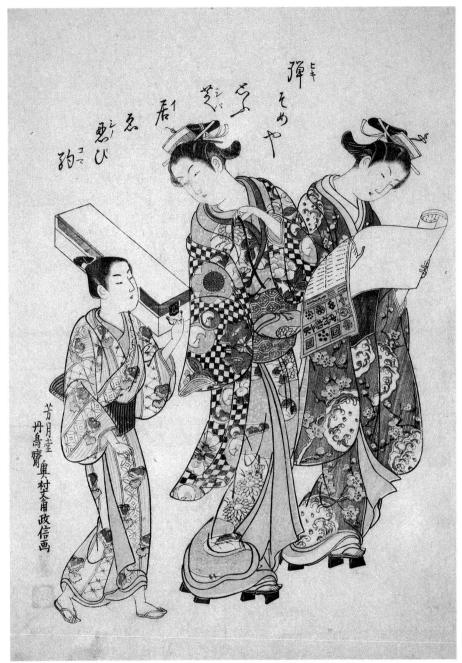

29

30

31

32

NISHIMURA SHIGENAGA
d. 1756

31 *The actor Sanjō Kantarō as a tea-seller*
Published by Igaya
c. 1716–36
Woodblock with hand-colouring and 'lacquer' (ink and glue), 328
    × 159 mm
1906.12-20.49

The actor represents a travelling seller of Uji tea. She
carries in her baskets a brazier, jars of tea, and teabowls
with which she could brew samples for customers. The
print is signed 'The brush of the Japanese craft-artist
Nishimura Shigenaga'.

NISHIMURA SHIGENOBU
Worked 1730–41

32 *A scene from a New Year Kabuki play*
    on the Soga Brothers
Published by Urokogataya Magobei
1732
Woodblock with hand-colouring, 'lacquer' (ink and glue) and
    metal dust, 316 × 151 mm
1906.12-20.48

The actors are Ichikawa Danjūrō II as a demon king and
Sadojima Chōgorō as Soga Jūrō. Plays on the medieval
story of the revenge of the Soga Brothers were frequently
performed at New Year. Jūrō is shown making an
offering at a shrine. The print is signed 'The artist
Nishimura Magosaburō'.

KATSUMURA TERUNOBU
Worked *c.* 1716–36

33 *The actor Yamamura Ichitarō in a female part*
Published by Igaya
1721–3
Woodblock with hand-colouring, 'lacquer' (ink and glue) and
    metal dust, 305 × 155 mm
1932.2-23.01

Ichitarō, a noted female impersonator, came up to Edo
(Tokyo) from Osaka in 1721. The New Year symbols
on his outer dress, including decorated battledores,
pine-fronds and a rice-cake on an offering-stand,
indicate that the print was issued at that time of year. It is
signed 'Katsumura Terunobu'.

33

ISHIKAWA TOYONOBU
1711–85

34 *A Korean smoking*

c. 1741–8
Woodblock, 667 × 150 mm
1906.12-20.45

The Korean, recognisable from his tall hat, is
shown smoking. The smoke forms seven
characters from a Chinese poem of the Tang
Dynasty. As in the print by Kiyonobu (no. 23),
there may be some confusion between Chinese
and Koreans, whom the Japanese of the time
never normally saw because of their
Government's policy of Isolation. The print is
sealed 'Ishikawa-shi' and 'Toyonobu'.

ISHIKAWA TOYONOBU

35 *The young actor Bandō Kikumatsu with a*
hobby-horse

Published by Maruya Shōbei
c. 1751–64
Woodblock, 430 × 303 mm
1907.5-31.7

The child-actor assumed the prestigious title of
'Second-Generation Hikosaburō' in 1751. The
hobby-horse is used in a spring dance, but the
chrysanthemums in the background suggest that
this was an autumn event. The inscription refers
to the actor's great promise. This is one of the
finest *benizurie* – prints done with pink and green
blocks as well as black outline. It is signed 'Picture
by Ishikawa Shūen Toyonobu' and sealed 'Ishikawa-shi'
and 'Toyonobu'.

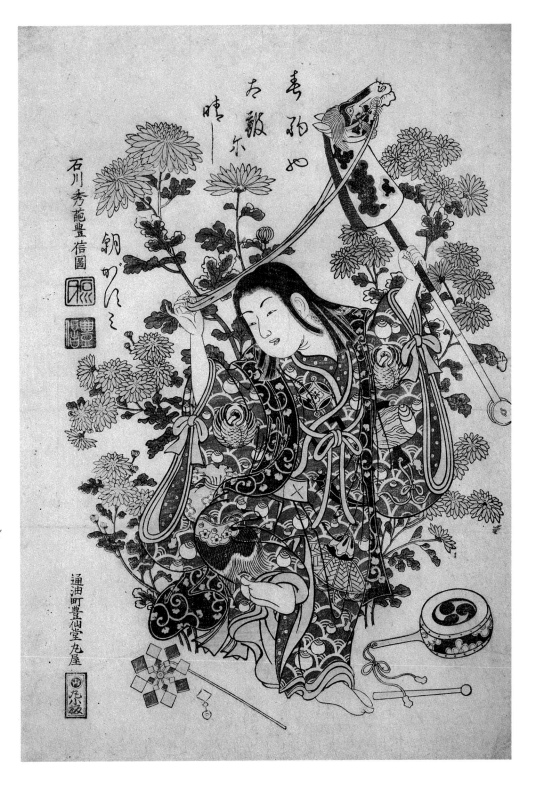

ISHIKAWA TOYONOBU

36 *The Four Accomplishments*
Published by Urokogataya Magobei
c. 1760–5
Woodblock, 305 × 430 mm
1923.7-16.017

This is a *mitate*, or travesty, of the classic Chinese four gentlemanly accomplishments of music, chess, calligraphy and painting. Music is represented by the *koto* (a horizontal harp) and Chinese chess by the more popular board-game of *go* (bottom left). The folding screen (top left) is decorated with plum blossom, indicating that it is early spring. The inscription suggests that the boys and girls find the accomplishments more enjoyable than the 'flowers' (the beautiful women instructing them). More than two colours are printed, consistent with the date attributed. The print is signed 'Painted by Ishikawa Shūen'.

TANAKA MASUNOBU
Worked 1740s

37 *The novelist Murasaki Shikibu*
c. 1744–8
Woodblock with hand-colouring, 298 × 419 mm
1906.12-20.39

This is an *ukie* (perspective print) using a modified form of the European convention of the vanishing-point. Japan's most famous writer, author of *Genji Monogatari* ('The Tale of Genji', *c.* AD 1000), is shown looking out from the Ishiyama Temple on Lake Biwa, where tradition has it she wrote the work. Seven of the 'Eight Views of Lake Biwa' are noted in the inscriptions in the background. The eighth – *Evening Bell at Ishiyama Temple* – is the subject of the foreground. The signature Tanaka Masunobu is on the *tsuitate* (standing screen) behind Murasaki.

MANGETSUDŌ
Worked 1740s

38 *Dreaming of aubergines*
Published by Emiya Kichiemon
c. 1744–8
Woodblock, 301 × 146 mm
1931.5-13.05

This is the right-hand sheet of a set of three on the subject of the 'Three Lucky Dreams'. They are *Mount Fuji*, *Two Hawks* and *Three Aubergines*.

A young woman puts a pin in her hair while looking at a hand-mirror. The aubergines are painted on the sliding-door behind her. Outside is a water-stoop with a ladle. The print is signed 'Mangetsudō' and sealed 'Kōrin' (alternatively 'Benirin'). There is no connection with the celebrated painter Ogata Kōrin (1652–1716).

TORII KIYOMITSU
1735–85

39 *Actors as Ohana and Hanshichi*
Published by Nishimuraya Yohachi
1765
Woodblock, 438 × 307 mm
1907.5-31.1

This was the second feature on the bill at the Nakamura-za Kabuki theatre in Edo (Tokyo) at New Year, 1765. On the left is the female impersonator Segawa Kikunojō as Ohana, and on the right Nakamura Matsue as Hanshichi. The play was based on the medieval story of the Soga Brothers' revenge, often performed at New Year. The actors' crests are shown above; the print is signed 'Painted by Torii Kiyomitsu' and sealed 'Kiyomitsu'.

TORII KIYOMITSU

40 *Young actors as ?Ohana and Hanshichi*
Published by Nishimuraya Yōhachi
1764–5
Woodblock, 435 × 315 mm
1935.12-14.02

The rising young players are (left) Bandō Hikosaburō and (right) Arashi Hinatsugu, thought to be acting the lovers Ohana and Hanshichi, one of the most popular stories of the Kabuki theatre. The actors' crests are shown above. The print is signed 'Painted by Torii Kiyomitsu' and sealed 'Kiyomitsu'.

TORII KIYOMITSU

41 *Pulling the boat*
Published by Nishimuraya Yohachi
c. 1762–8
Woodblock, 300 × 138 mm
1945.11-1.045

This is a *mizue* (water picture). These very delicately printed pictures were done in light colours without outline and had a short vogue at this period. They were the predecessors of the *surimono* reproduced in the last section of this book (see nos 188–200). It is thought that the mountain is Tsukubayama and that the scene is the dividing point of the Ayase and Hikibune Rivers. A poem by the eleventh-century poetess Eifuku Mon'in is quoted top left. The print is signed 'Painted by Torii Kiyomitsu'.

40

41

TORII KIYOMITSU

42 *Courtesans of the Three Cities*

Published by Iwatoya Gempachi
c. 1762–8
Woodblock, 285 × 421 mm
1906.12-20.23

This three-sheet composition was designed to be
cut up; if it is not, the 'right' and 'left' are the
wrong way round, as in this example.
Comparisons of the beauties of the 'Three Cities'
were extremely popular among the men of Edo
(Tokyo), who were fascinated by the older
traditions of Osaka and Kyoto. Here the
courtesans' attendants carry battledores marked
(left) Osaka, (centre) Edo and (right) Miyako =
Kyoto. The inscriptions fancifully compare them
to the beauties of spring. The comparatively early
date of this and the following print is suggested
by the simple colour scheme. The left-hand
section is signed 'Painted by Torii Kiyomitsu'.

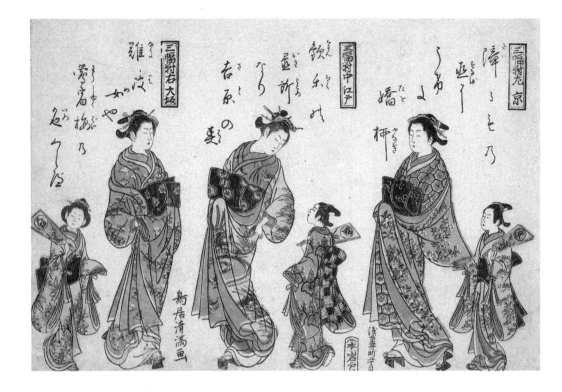

ANON

43 *A pleasure-boat on the Sumida River*

c. 1705–15
Woodblock with some hand-colouring, 317 × 463 mm
1945.11-1.01

The scene is by the Ryōgoku Bridge on the
Sumida River in Edo (Tokyo). On the left is a ferry
to the Yoshiwara brothel district.

ANON (?TORII KIYOMITSU 1735–85)

44 *The actors Ichikawa Danjūrō II and Sanogawa Mangiku*

1719
Woodblock with hand-colouring, 212 × 107 mm (each)
1929.6-11.03

This composition would have been designed to be cut and separated down the centre. The scene is probably from a performance of the Kabuki play *Soga-Saki Shinchū* at the Nakamura-za theatre in Edo (Tokyo). Danjūrō (right) plays Tokubei and Mangiku (left) plays Ohatsu. They are in a tea-house at the Kamedo shrine, where Ohatsu is serving.

ANON

45 *The actor Ichikawa Danjūrō II in a part*

1721
Woodblock with hand-colouring, 'lacquer' (ink and glue) and metal dust, 327 × 155 mm
1906.12-20.20

The role is thought to be that of Yojirōbei in a New Year's play on the theme of the Soga Brothers' revenge at the Morita-za theatre in Edo (Tokyo). The straw hat is traditionally worn by a hero in disguise. The long text is a quotation from the play as actually performed on that occasion.

TORII KIYOTADA
Worked *c.* 1720–50

46 *The Daimonjiya Brothel*
Published by Okumuraya Sadamura
c. 1745–50
Woodblock with hand-colouring, 477 × 690 mm
1922.12-14.09

This is an *ukie* (perspective print) using European perspective, in this case in an exaggerated way. The scene is one of the greatest houses of courtesans in the Shin Yoshiwara licensed district of Edo (Tokyo). The inhabitants are seen smoking, playing the board-game of *sugoroku* and performing music. The print is signed 'The brush of the artist Torii Kiyotada'.

ANON

47 *A scene from the Karakuri theatre*
c. 1770
Woodblock, 263 × 400 mm
1973.7-23.014

This is a reprint of a work of the 1740s, which accounts for the very limited colours used. From the original it is known to show a scene in a brothel from the *Karakuri* (mechanical doll) theatre. This novelty entertainment was especially in vogue at the time.

?SUMIYOSHI SCHOOL

48 *Spring scenes in Ueno*
c. 1720
Handscroll, ink, colours and gold on paper, 295 mm ×
    11 m (approx.)
1950.11-11.021

This long handscroll and the following were the
first of what were originally a set of four depicting
scenes in Edo (Tokyo) in spring, summer, autumn
and winter; only these two survive. Ueno, a hilly
district in the north of Edo, included the
Shinobazu pond, the Tōshogū shrines devoted to
the Shogun's family and the Kan'ei Temple. The
scene is dominated by merrymaking at
cherry-blossom time, a festival still
enthusiastically observed in Ueno. The brilliance
possible in painting, well demonstrated in this
scroll, gave the impetus to its imitation in
full-colour printing.

?SUMIYOSHI SCHOOL

49 *Summer scenes in Asakusa*

c. 1720
Handscroll, ink, colours and gold on paper, 295 mm ×
   11 m (approx.)
1950.11-11.022

Asakusa was an area of popular resort by the
Sumida River, centring on the Ryōgoku Bridge
and the Asakusa Kannon Temple. It was and
remains famous for its shops and entertainments,
which are here described in great detail.

The Birth of the Full Colour Print

SUZUKI HARUNOBU 1724–70

50 *Clearing storm at Asakusa*
1764–70
Woodblock, 280 × 212 mm
1960.7-16.03

This is from a set of 'Eight Views of Contemporary Edo' (Tokyo), each based on a theme from the classical Chinese set known as 'Eight Views of the Xiaoxiang Rivers'. The scene is a toothbrush stall behind the Asakusa Kannon Temple. A young samurai, his head hooded as a disguise, is entertained by the celebrated shop-girl Ofuji. Fallen ginkgo leaves show that it is autumn. The print is signed 'Painted by Suzuki Harunobu'.

SUZUKI HARUNOBU

51 *Returning sails at Shinagawa*
1764–70
Woodblock, 291 × 213 mm
1937.7-10.015

From the series 'Eight Views of Today's Floating World', based on the classical Chinese set of 'Eight Views of the Xiaoxiang Rivers'. A prostitute down the coast at Shinagawa in the early morning watches the returning boats which have taken the clients back to Edo. Like many of Harunobu's prints, it is accompanied by a thirty-one-syllable poem. The print is signed 'Painted by Suzuki Harunobu'.

SUZUKI HARUNOBU

52 *The Eirakuan Tea-house*
1764–70
Woodblock, 278 × 199 mm
1902.2-12.170

This is thought to be a tea-house at Gion, the centre of
the entertainment quarter in Kyoto. A senior maid is
carrying warmed saké to a client who can be seen in an
inner room. A junior maid seems to be warming saké in
the corridor. The characters '. . . rakuan' can be seen on
the paper lantern above the stone lantern. The space for
a poem above has not been filled. The print is signed
'Painted by Harunobu'.

SUZUKI HARUNOBU

53 *A travesty of 'The Hundred Poets'*
1764–70
Woodblock, 278 × 207 mm
1937.7-10.046

As a result of his success with printed calendars, Harunobu did many
prints based on Japan's classical literature in *mitate*, or travesty, form.
This example recreates in contemporary terms poem no. 14 from the
thirteenth-century anthology *Ogura Hyakunin Isshū*. The poem by
Kawahara no Sadaijin includes a reference to the emotional effect of
multi-coloured textiles. A young woman listens enraptured to the
drum of an effeminate young man in the moonlight. A love-letter is
tied to the bush-clover, symbol of autumnal melancholy. The print is
signed 'Painted by Suzuki Harunobu'.

SUZUKI HARUNOBU

54 *The Yamabuki by the Water*

1766–8
Woodblock, 356 × 264 mm
1945.11-1.07

A servant hands to a woman crossing river-shallows a
branch of *yamabuki* (kerria). The poem, from the
anthology *Shin Shui Wakashū*, is by Motouji and can be
rendered: 'On the flowing waters of the Kawase River,
appearing as reflections, the *kerria* flowers float but have
not fallen.' Here the apprentice hands a *kerria* branch to
the courtesan, who is reflected in the water. The print is
signed 'Painted by Harunobu'.

SUZUKI HARUNOBU

55 *The poetess Ono no Komachi*

1764–70
Woodblock with blind-printing, 273 × 200 mm
1906.12-20.62

This elegant print is in fact a full-colour plagiarism from
the black and white book *Ehon Tokiwagusa* by Nishikawa
Sukenobu (1671–1750). The background shows traces of
the original blue pigment, which has almost entirely
faded. The semi-legendary ninth-century poetess is
shown in a many-layered court dress.

SUZUKI HARUNOBU

56 *Flirtation*
1764–70
Woodblock, 198 × 313 mm
1906.12-20.79

A young couple dally on the veranda,
overlooking a stream with the moon
reflected in it. The flowering bush-clover
shows that it is autumn. An older
woman watches from behind the
sliding partition. She is perhaps a
go-between, perhaps a brothel madam;
probably in Harunobu's disarmingly
innocent world she is both. The print is
signed 'Painted by Harunobu'.

SUZUKI HARUNOBU

57 *Travesty of Ono no Michikaze*
1768–70
Woodblock (pillar print), 662 × 116 mm
1907.5-31.348

The tenth-century poet Ono no
Michikaze once watched a frog
climbing a willow on a rainy day and
compared it to the painful way
success is gained. Harunobu turns
the story into a young woman
longing for success in love. The print
is signed 'Painted by Harunobu'.

57

58

59

60

SUZUKI HARUNOBU

58 *The Kinuta River*

1768–70
Woodblock (pillar print), 666 × 110 mm
1907.5-31.351

This is from a series 'The Six Crystal Rivers Up-to-date', based on an ancient Japanese set of river-subjects used in both literature and art. A prostitute comes on to the veranda in her night attire. The long poem-slip above her head gives the series title and quotes a poem of autumnal melancholy. Next to it is a poem card (listed in the card game of the 'Hundred Poets') which identifies the Kinuta River in Settsu Province above a portrait of a classical poetess. The print is signed 'Painted by Harunobu'.

YAMAMOTO FUJINOBU
Worked 1751–72

59 *A fan-seller*

c. 1770
Woodblock (pillar print), 700 × 116 mm
1920.5-14.015

A modish-looking young man is watched from a bamboo grille by a courtesan. He is carrying a box of fan-papers. The print is signed 'Painted by Fujinobu'.

SEIGYŪ GYŌCHIN
Worked *c.* 1751–64

60 *The raconteur Shidōken*

Published by Tomita
?*c.* 1760
Woodblock (pillar print), 668 × 97 mm
OA + 062

The 'crossroads lecturer' Shidoken sits in the Asakusa Kannon Temple precincts. He makes his points by banging on his desk with a wooden phallus. Shidoken specialised in war stories. The print is signed 'Painted by Seigyū Gyōchin'.

SHIBA KŌKAN 1747–1818

61 *Travesty of Ono no Komachi praying for rain*
1771–2
Woodblock, 370 × 192 mm
1914.4-7.03

This is from a series, 'The Seven Komachis Up-to-date', in which the seven famous events in the life of the semi-legendary ninth-century poetess are aped. Here the subject is Komachi's praying for rain during a drought. In the upper room of a brothel overlooking the embankment leading to the Yoshiwara district a prostitute grooms a young client, while an attendant boils the water for tea. Shiba Kōkan designed some prints in the style of Harunobu; this print is signed 'Painted by Harushige'.

Attributed to
SHIBA KŌKAN

62 *A Bugaku Dancer*

1788
Woodblock, 142 × 103 mm
1968.2-12.026

This is a calendar print for 1788; the numbers of the 'long' and 'short' months of the lunar calendar, which was very complex and changed every year, are concealed in the robes of the dancer. *Bugaku* was a courtly dance-drama which flourished in the Middle Ages. There was a revival of interest in it in the eighteenth century.

SHIBA KŌKAN

63 *Tōbōsaku and the peach*

c. 1790
Woodblock, 126 × 192 mm
1968.2-12.025

This is probably a calendar print, concealing in the design the numbers of the 'long' and 'short' months of the lunar calendar. In Chinese Daoist legend Tōbōsaku stole the peach from the Immortal Seiōbō and achieved longevity. The print is signed 'Copied by Kōkan Shiba Shun'.

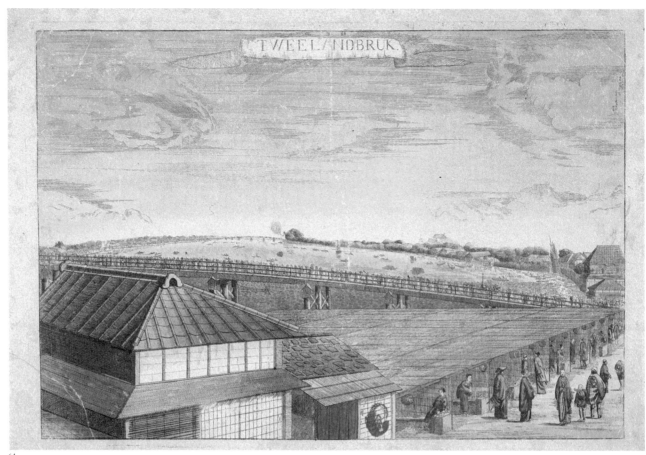

64

65

SHIBA KŌKAN

64 *The Ryōgoku Bridge*
Published by the artist
1787
Hand-coloured etching, 285 × 418 mm
1949.11-12.010

Kōkan is credited with producing Japan's first
etching in 1783, a technique learned from a
manual brought by the Dutch traders to Nagasaki.
This is a view of the Ryōgoku Bridge at Asakusa in
Edo (Tokyo). It is designed for a magic lantern and
is therefore reversed. The title is the Dutch for
'Ryōgoku Bridge'. The inscription at the top is
dated the ninth month of Temmei Seventh Year
(1787) and states that Shiba Kōkan himself etched
the plates, the first artist in Japan to do so.

SHIBA KŌKAN

65 *A farmer*
c. 1800
Hanging scroll, ink and light colours on silk,
  260 × 634 mm
1913.5-1.0352

In his later years Kōkan tried to combine
European and East Asian painting techniques,
using his native materials combined with
European artistic conventions. The painting is
signed 'Copied by Kōkan Shiba Shun'. The seals
read 'Shiba' and 'Shun'.

66

67

ISODA KORYŪSAI
Worked 1764–89

66 *Reading interrupted*
c. 1770
Woodblock (pillar print), 672 × 118 mm
1907.5-31.372

A young courtesan reads a book of *nagauta*
(narrative poems). Her lover dangles a
small toy from behind a bamboo grille.
The print is signed 'Painted by Koryū'.

ISODA KORYŪSAI

67 *Returning sails in the hand-basin*
c. 1775
Woodblock (pillar print), 682 × 115 mm
1907.5-31.364

This is from a set entitled 'Eight Views of
Fashionable Mansions' (that is, brothels). It
relates the classic Chinese 'Eight Views of
the Xiaoxiang Rivers' to ordinary domestic
objects. In this case a hanging hand-towel
over a basin recalls the 'returning sails'
subject. Two young women have made a
boat of bamboo leaves to float on the basin.
The print is signed 'Painted by Koryūsai'.

ISODA KORYŪSAI

68 First dream of the year

c. 1775
Woodblock (double pillar print), 680 × 118 mm (each)
1908.4-14.1064

This is a very rare example of two pillar prints
which fit together. They were intended to be
mounted as cheap hanging scrolls and hung side
by side. A young woman and man are shown
with the 'Three Lucky Dreams' – *Mount Fuji, (Two)
Hawks* and *Three Aubergines*. The prints are signed
'Painted by Koryūsai'.

68

ISODA KORYŪSAI

69 *First dream of the year*

c. 1775
Woodblock (pillar print), 671 × 105 mm
1907.5-31.369

A prostitute has fallen asleep while writing a letter. She dreams the 'Three Lucky Dreams' – *Mount Fuji*, *Two Hawks* and *Three Aubergines*. The peacock designs on her outer garment, the transparent fan and the Chinese-style writing equipment all suggest a reference to the Chinese Immortal who dreamt of a butterfly dreaming of him. The print is signed 'Painted by Koryūsai'.

ISODA KORYŪSAI

70 *Travesty of Lady Murasaki*

c. 1775
Woodblock (pillar print), 675 × 121 mm
1902.2-12.175

A young man of fashion sits on the veranda of a brothel at Shinagawa, overlooking Edo (Tokyo) Bay. He is holding a writing-brush. This is a reference to Lady Murasaki, author of *Genji Monogatari* ('The Tale of Genji', *c.* AD 1000) sitting in the Ishiyama Temple on Lake Biwa. The pine-tree and setting sun are often shown in this scene. Koryūsai has designed the horizon with a curve. The print is signed 'Painted by Koryū'.

ISODA KORYŪSAI

71 *Inside and outside the mosquito net*

c. 1781
Woodblock (pillar print), 690 × 115 mm
1921.4-11.03

A woman under a mosquito net pursues insects with a taper. A young man is about to intrude. The print is sealed 'Yagenbori', apparently Koryūsai's own district.

69

70

71

ISODA KORYŪSAI

72 *Dragon and tiger*

c. 1780
Woodblock with some hand-colouring,
779 × 274 mm
1914.2-17.01

The dragon (with clouds and sea) and
tiger (with bamboo) are both common
Buddhist symbols. This very rare print,
using techniques derived from stone-
rubbing, would have been made as a
substitute hanging painting in the style
of the official Kanō School. It is signed
'Painted by Koryū'.

Attributed to
ISODA KORYŪSAI

73 *Hawks, peonies and torrents*

c. 1781
Woodblock, with some hand-colouring,
803 × 290 mm
1958.7-12.015

This is another poor man's hanging
scroll done in the style of the official
Kanō School. It too uses techniques
derived from stone-rubbing. The
attribution to Koryūsai is almost certain,
although there is no signature.

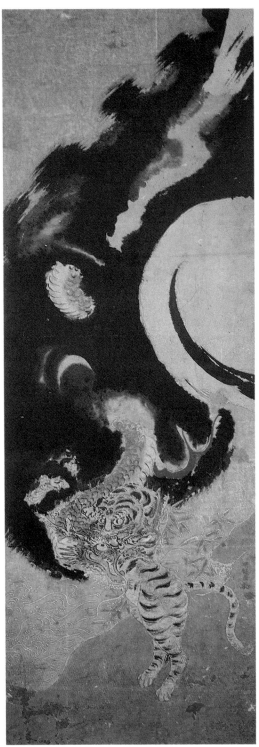

72

73

The Golden Age

TORII KIYONAGA 1752–1815

74 *The Bush-Clover Garden*

1783–4
Woodblock (diptych print), 385 × 260 mm (each)
1924.3-27.08

The splendid set 'Brocades of Fashion of the East' consists of one- or two-sheet prints of the pleasurable world of Edo (Tokyo). With such prints Kiyonaga initiated the 'golden age' of *Ukiyoe*, his tall, statuesque figures becoming the ideal. Here a young samurai in formal attire is attended by a tea-girl in the garden at the Ryōganji Temple at Kamedo. On the right three women from the entertainment quarter ogle him. The two sheets are signed 'Painted by Kiyonaga'.

75

76

77

TORII KIYONAGA

75 *Asukayama at Cherry-blossom time*

c. 1785
Woodblock (triptych print), 370 × 255 mm (each)
1906.12-20.220

This splendidly broad *plein-air* composition is a
landmark in the development of the *Ukiyoe* print.
For the first time European pictorial conventions
had been thoroughly and effortlessly integrated
into a relaxed synthesis. Similarly, different
classes from Japan's codified society meet almost
face-to-face to admire the cherry-blossom at one of
Edo's favourite spots. On the left the daughter of
a *daimyō* (feudal lord) is led by her nurses. On the
right are shop-girls and other townswomen. The
print is signed 'Painted by Kiyonaga'.

TORII KIYONAGA

76 *A pleasure-boat on the Sumida River*

c. 1785–8
Woodblock (triptych print), 390 × 250 mm (each)
1927.6-13.020

A scene typical of Edo (Tokyo) *Ukiyoe*: actors with
courtesans and entertainers are carried on the
river, while lesser townspeople crowd in small
boats to try to see them. On board a trained
monkey dances to the music of *shamisen*
(three-stringed guitars) and drums. The print is
signed 'Painted by Kiyonaga'.

TORII KIYONAGA

77 *Women visiting Enoshima*

Published by Nishimuraya Yōhachi
c. 1785–8
Woodblock (triptych print), 370 × 245 mm (each)
1906.12-20.221

The island of Enoshima near Kamakura was
within easy reach of Edo (Tokyo). It had a fine
view of Mount Fuji, and the shrine on the island
to Benzaiten (a patron of wealth and music) was
particularly popular with women, who could
combine a trip with devotion. The island could be
reached by foot at low tide. Kiyonaga's big
populated views are the predecessors of the true
landscape prints of fifty years later. The print is
signed 'Painted by Kiyonaga'.

78   79   80

TORII KIYONAGA

78 *Mother and child, with a toy dog*

c. 1780
Woodblock (pillar print), 698 × 124 mm
1931.5-13.025

A shaven-headed boy pulls his mother's kimono
and asks for the toy dog she is holding. The
cricket-cage hung outside shows that it is hot
weather. The print is signed 'Painted by
Kiyonaga'.

TORII KIYONAGA

79 *Actors doing the spring dance*

Published by Nishimuraya Yohachi
1782
Woodblock (pillar print), 667 × 116 mm
1906.12-20.217

The actors, riding hobby-horses, are Segawa
Kikunojō III and Iwai Hanshirō IV. They are
performing an extract from the drama
Mutsumashitsuki Koi no Tedori ('The Profit of New
Year's Love') recited by the *jōruri* (dramatic
narrative) master Tomimoto Buzen-dayu. The
print is signed 'Painted by Kiyonaga'.

TORII KIYONAGA

80 *Two women and a child at night*

Published by Nishimuraya Yohachi
c. 1785
Woodblock (pillar print), 610 × 118 mm
1925.4-6.06

It is a summer night. The device of using a black
background to represent night is remarkably rare
among *Ukiyoe* prints. The print is signed 'Painted
by Kiyonaga'.

KITAGAWA UTAMARO 1753–1806

81 *Colours and scents of flowers of the four seasons*

Published by Tsutaya Jūsaburō
c. 1784
Woodblock (diptych print), 375 × 250 mm (each)
1945.11-1.047

A very elegant young man, accompanied by women, lounges on a pleasure-boat on the Sumida River.
Women from the entertainment quarter come to the quay to join him. This apparently unique copy shows
the early development of Utamaro's style, still influenced by Shigemasa and Kiyonaga but already with a
flavour of its own, particularly in the male figure. The woman looking through gauze became one of
his favourite devices. The print is signed 'Painted by Utamaro'.

KITAGAWA UTAMARO

82 *Drying clothes*

Published by Iwatoya Kisaburō
c. 1785–90
Woodblock (two sheets of a triptych print), 372 × 242 mm (each)
1909.6-18.83

The missing left-hand sheet showed an interior. Women are drying clothes on an Edo (Tokyo) rooftop, looking south-west to the distant Mount Fuji. The cuckoo indicates it is early summer. The print is signed 'Painted by Utamaro'.

KITAGAWA UTAMARO

83 *A feast in a 'Chinese' brothel*

Published by Tsutaya Jūsaburō
?1790
Woodblock (triptych print), 365 × 240 mm (each)
1909.6-18.84

A fanciful reconstruction of a Chinese house of courtesans, but in fact populated by typical Utamaro women in only slightly modified dress. The background scenery is in the style of the official Kanō School which Utamaro both despised and envied. The print was probably published to coincide with an embassy from the Ryūkyū Islands in 1790. Japanese of the time perceived the Ryūkyūans as 'Chinese'. It is signed 'Painted by Utamaro'.

82

83

KITAGAWA UTAMARO

84 *A poet's success*

Published by Tsutaya Jūsaburō
c. 1788–90
Woodblock (diptych print), 390 × 255 mm (each)
1922.7-19.02

This scene of a tourist trip down the coast to Matsubara near Mount Fuji celebrates the entry of the *kyōka* (comic verse) poet Shūrakusai Takimaro into the poetic circle led by Ōta Nampo. Takimaro is in the front *kago* (carrying chair). Poems by Nampo and two other club leaders are printed above. The print is signed 'Painted by Utamaro'.

KITAGAWA UTAMARO

85 *A travesty of the 'Six Poets'*

Published by Tsutaya Jūsaburō
c. 1790
Woodblock (diptych print), 367 × 239 mm (each)
1906.12-20.354

The six most famous Japanese poets (all of the ninth century) are shown with their traditional attributes but in the form of six beautiful women of the day. The women are identified above with the appropriate poems. On the right is Ohisa, one of Utamaro's favourite subjects. The print is signed 'Painted by Utamaro'.

KITAGAWA UTAMARO

86 *Dancers from the Niwaka Festival*
Published by Tsuruya Kiemon
c. 1792
Woodblock with powdered mica ground, 392 × 260 mm
1931.5-13.021

This is one of a series of four showing the great dance
festival held in August in the Shin Yoshiwara, the major
licensed pleasure quarter of Edo (Tokyo). The characters,
played by Young geisha, are a 'Chinese', a lion-dog and
the wrestler Kānshū. The print is signed 'Painted by
Utamaro'.

KITAGAWA UTAMARO

87 *The male geisha Ogie Matsuzō*
Published by Tsutaya Jūsaburō
c. 1792
Woodblock, 380 × 252 mm
1924.3-27.014

A procession during the Niwaka Festival, a street dance festival
happening in August in the Shin Yoshiwara, the major licensed
entertainment quarter in Edo (Tokyo). Butterflies and peonies
specially decorated this summer event. The male geisha Matsuzō
(identified on his fan) is accompanied by two female geisha –
Ito and Mine. The print is signed 'The brush of Utamaro'.

KITAGAWA UTAMARO

88 *Front and back views of*
Ohisa

c. 1792
Woodblock (printed both sides),
325 × 147 mm
1945.11-1.021

Utamaro's favourite beauty,
Ohisa of the Tea-house of
Takashima, is given the
accolade of both front and
back views in this very rare
print. The signature is
'Painted by Utamaro'.

KITAGAWA UTAMARO

89 *The Beauty Ohisa*
Published by Tsutaya Jūsaburō
c. 1792–3
Woodblock, 376 × 247 mm
1927.6-13.06

The daughter of the tea-seller Takashimaya Chōbei near
the Ryōgoku Bridge in Edo (Tokyo), Ohisa was the most
celebrated beauty and hostess of the time. The poem on
a representation of a decorated paper *tanzaku* (poem-slip)
refers to her floral crest. The print is signed 'The brush of
Utamaro'.

KITAGAWA UTAMARO

90 *The fickle type*
Published by Tsutaya Jūsaburō
c. 1792–3
Woodblock with powdered mica ground, 350 × 247 mm
1945.11-1.018

The best-known of the incomplete set 'Ten Female
Faces', and one of Utamaro's erotic masterpieces. Her
kimono was probably originally a pale blue, the
vegetable dye having changed colour through its own
chemical action. The print is signed 'Painted by
Utamaro'.

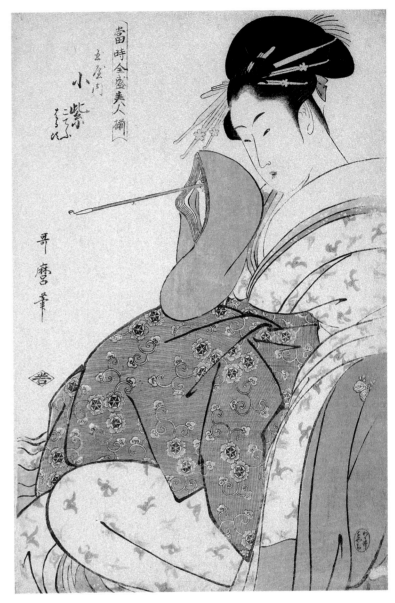

KITAGAWA UTAMARO

91 *Yearning for her lover*
Published by Tsutaya Jūsaburō
c. 1793
Woodblock with tinted powdered mica ground, 383 × 251 mm
1906.12-20.331

A young woman who rarely meets her lover, from the
series 'Six Selected Types of Love'. The title of the series
punningly refers to Utamaro's name and to the six
classical poets of the ninth century. The print is signed
'The brush of Utamaro'.

KITAGAWA UTAMARO

92 *The courtesan Komurasaki*
Published by Wakasaya Yoichi
c. 1794
Woodblock, 384 × 252 mm
1924.3-27.015

This is one of the series 'A Set of the Great Beauties of the Day'
and shows the prostitute Komurasaki of the House of Tamaya.
Utamaro depicts her almost pouring out of the composition
at the viewer, possibly a reference to her strong effect on her clients.
The vegetable blue of the original has changed colour under
its own chemical action. The print is signed 'The brush of Utamaro'.

KITAGAWA UTAMARO

93 *The artist with friends*
Published by Ōmiya Gonkurō
1795–1800
Woodblock (one sheet of a diptych print), 362 × 268 mm
1922.2-13.06

A travesty of the eleventh scene of the Kabuki play *Chūshingura* ('The Loyal League'), from the series 'The Chūshingura Travestied by Today's Great Beauties'. The last scene is a two-sheet print, of which this is the left. In it Utamaro shows himself as one of the play's male characters, surrounded by his adored women. The signature on the pillar reads 'By request, Utamaro himself copied these charming figures'.

KITAGAWA UTAMARO

94 *The bath-robe*
Published by Tsuruya Kiemon
c. 1797
Woodblock, 377 × 254 mm
1914.4-7.04

This is from a set entitled 'New Brocade Patterns in Utamaro's Style'. The flowered bath-robe is printed without outline. The title cartouche is in the form of a handscroll and includes a manifesto by Utamaro on his own excellence. The signature is 'The brush of Utamaro'.

KITAGAWA UTAMARO

95 *The outer-robe*
Published by Tsuruya Kiemon
c. 1797
Woodblock, 373 × 250 mm
1906.12-20.346

This also is from the set entitled 'New Brocade Patterns in Utamaro's Style'. The white *uchikake* (outer robe) is left in the white of the paper. No outline is used in the woman's clothes. The title cartouche is in the form of a handscroll, and is used by Utamaro to claim that he is superior to his rivals as a portrayer of women. The print is signed 'The brush of Utamaro'.

KITAGAWA UTAMARO

96 *Women on the Ryōgoku Bridge*
Published by Ōmiya Gonkurō
1795–1800
Woodblock (three prints of six), 365 × 250 mm (each)
1918.7-5.01-03

This is the top three sections of a composition of
six sheets; the lower half showed the scene under
the bridge. On the left are attendants of the great,
in the centre townswomen, and on the right
entertainers. The print is signed 'The brush of
Utamaro'.

KITAGAWA UTAMARO

97 *Night on the River*

1795–1800
Woodblock (triptych print), 370 × 240 mm (each)
1910.6-14.16

On a hot summer night rich revellers disport on a
pleasure-boat on the Sumida River in Edo
(Tokyo). They have drawn up by a fishing boat to
watch it. The print is signed 'The brush of
Utamaro'.

KITAGAWA UTAMARO

98 *Going down to the East*

Published by Moriya Jihei
1795–1800
Woodblock (triptych print), 370 × 245 mm (each)
1906.12-20.364

This is a travesty of the ninth chapter of the classic
work of Japanese literature *Ise Monogatari* ('Tales
of Ise'). In it the exiled poet Narihira stops near
Mount Fuji to admire it. Here the scene is played
by contemporary men and women. The men are
imitating court dress. The signature is 'The brush
of Utamaro'.

KITAGAWA UTAMARO

99 *The lovers Chūbei and Umegawa*

Published by Ōmiya Gonkurō
1795–1800
Woodblock, 343 × 242 mm
1920.2-17.04

This is from a series called 'Eight Views of Ōmi' showing eight classic subjects derived from a Chinese set on the Xiaoxiang Rivers. In this case the subject is *Returning Sails*, and the scene is on Lake Biwa near Kyoto. All this is in the cartouche (top left). The true subject is the celebrated story of the eloping lovers Chūbei and Umegawa, a favourite of the townspeople of the time. The signature is 'The brush of Utamaro'.

KITAGAWA UTAMARO

100 *The lovers Osome and Hisamatsu frustrated*

Published by Yamaguchiya Chūsuke
1795–1800
Woodblock, 382 × 257 mm
1924.1-15.024

From the series 'A Mirror of Flirting Lovers' depicting sad stories of urban love. The true story happened about 1708, when the son of an oil-merchant (shown here in spectacles) fell in love with a girl disapproved of by the father. The interfering old man is the 'cloud over the moon' of the second part of the series title. The print is signed 'The brush of Utamaro'.

KITAGAWA UTAMARO

101 *Drawing water for breakfast*

Published by Izumiya Ichibei
1795–1800
Woodblock with powdered mica ground, 372 × 255 mm
1937.7-10.068

This is from the series 'The Hours of the Day Among Ordinary Beauties'. Here at the Hour of the Rabbit in early morning two servant girls draw water from a well. Utamaro's passion for female beauty led him to explore every type, in spite of the then codified nature of Japanese society. The signature is 'The brush of Utamaro'.

101

KITAGAWA UTAMARO

102 *The seller of fans*

1795–1800
Woodblock (pillar print), 604 × 118 mm
1907.5-31.471

The seller of *uchiwa* (non-folding fans) is clearly
attractive to the woman, her youth betrayed by
her decorated hairpins. Some of the fans are
printed with figures in *Ukiyoe* style. The print is
signed 'The brush of Utamaro'.

KITAGAWA UTAMARO

103 *The lovers Chūbei and Umegawa*

Published by Murataya Jirobei
1795–1800
Woodblock (pillar print), 623 × 136 mm
1960.7-16.06

Utamaro has delighted in fitting the ill-starred
eloping lovers into the difficult pillar-print format.
He seemed to share with the Edo public a deep
delight in stories of conflicting duty and passion,
so inherent in the society of the time. The
signature is 'The brush of Utamaro'.

102

103

EISHŌSAI CHŌKI
Worked 1788–1809

104 *The courtesan Somenosuke with an apprentice*
Published by Tsutaya Jūsaburō
c. 1795
Woodblock, 350 × 252 mm
1931.5-13.017

One of two surviving prints from a series of half-length
portraits entitled 'A Collection of Beauties of the Green
Houses'. The 'Green Houses' were the great brothels of
the licensed Shin Yoshiwara district. Chōki's
'melon-shaped' faces were much admired at the time.
The print is signed 'The brush of Chōki'.

EISHŌSAI CHŌKI

105 *New Year Sunrise*
Published by Tsutaya Jūsaburō
c. 1795
Woodblock, 360 × 242 mm
1927.6-13.05

The New Year's sunrise was thought to be best watched
over the sea. The woman stands by a stone basin for
purification. By it the Fukujūsō plant also symbolises the
New Year. The print is signed 'Painted by Chōki'.

EISHŌSAI CHŌKI

106 *Catching fireflies*
Published by Tsutaya Jūsaburō
c. 1795
Woodblock with powdered black mica ground,
  382 × 250 mm
1945.11-1.044

One of the most celebrated of all *Ukiyoe* prints.
The irises show that it is May. The woman holds
a firefly cage, while the boy pursues the insects,
picked out in white on the black mica ground.
The print is signed 'Painted by Chōki'.

EISHŌSAI CHŌKI

107 *The Tea-house Beauty Okita*
Published by Yamadaya Sanshirō
1790–1800
Woodblock (pillar print), 610 × 113 mm
1915.6-1.04

Okita was one of the 'three beauties of the Kansei Era' (1789–1800). She was the *kambanmusume* or shopfront attraction of the Nambaya Tea-house. Here she is accompanied by a young woman with a toy dog. *Surimono* greeting cards are stuck to the wall behind her. The signature is 'Painted by Chōki'.

KINOSHITA SEKIJŌ
Worked 1789–1808

108 *Two courtesans*
c. 1795–1800
Woodblock (pillar print), 581 × 103 mm
1906.12-20.380

This little-known print artist has used a style close to Utamaro's. The prostitutes shown are Karauta (above) of the House of Chōjiya and Hanaogi of the House of Ogiya. The print is signed 'The brush of Sekijō'.

TAMAGAWA SHŪCHŌ
Worked *c.* 1789–1804

109 *The lovers Yūkiri and Izaemon*
1795–1800
Woodblock (pillar print), 621 × 118 mm
1907.5-31.481

Shūchō is a little-known artist. In this print he follows Utamaro's style to show the celebrated Osaka lovers Fujiya Izaemon and the prostitute Yūkiri. On her death in 1678 their story was made into a Kabuki play. The print is signed 'Painted by Shūchō'.

107

108

109

KUBO SHUMMAN 1757–1820

110 *The Shikian Restaurant*
Published by Shūeidō
c. 1787–8
Woodblock (diptych print), 363 × 253 mm
   (each)
1924.3-27.09

This famous two-storey restaurant
was on Nakazu, an artificial island in
the Sumida River in Edo (Tokyo)
which was later destroyed. A lucky *tai*
fish is being served. On the opposite
bank can be seen the storehouses of
Fukagawa. The print is signed
'Painted by Kubo Shumman'.

KUBO SHUMMAN

111 *The staff of the Nakadaya
     Restaurant*

c. 1787–8
Woodblock (triptych print), 320 × 220 mm
   (each)
1907.5-31.94

Shumman took this design from
Kiyonaga's book *Ehon Monomigaoka*
and rearranged it as a sheet-print
triptych. From the book it is known
that this is Nakadaya in the Mukōjima
district of Edo (Tokyo). In the centre a
performer plays the three-stringed
shamisen. Prints in this palette became
popular at the time. They were called
benigiraie ('pictures which hate red').
The signature is 'Painted by Kubo
Shumman'.

KUBO SHUMMAN

112 *A poetry meeting at night*

Published by Fushimiya Zenroku
c. 1787–8
Woodblock (triptych print), 375 × 255 mm (each)
1910.6-14.13

The scene is a very exclusive restaurant or private
house. In the upper room a priest and two
samurai are seen reading poetry. Another
participant is seen off by the staff. In a rare
attempt at naturalistic effects in *Ukiyoe* the artist
shows colour only where the light would pick it
up. As an active poet as well as an artist,
Shumman was well-qualified to record this world
where men and women of different classes could
mingle. The fullest of the signatures reads
'Painted by Shōsadō Kubo Shumman'.

113

KUBO SHUMMAN

113 From *The Six Crystal Rivers*
Published by Fushimiya Zenroku
c. 1787–8
Woodblock (three prints from a composition of six),
370 × 245 mm (each)
1910.2-12.438

The complete composition linked the six
famous rivers with a continuous
background. Each river is traditionally
associated with a subject which is depicted
again and again in Japanese art. Thus the
right-hand scene is the Kinuta River,
associated with beating cloth. Shumman
peoples these scenes with fashionable
women of his own day. The fullest of the
signatures is 'Painted by Kubo Shumman'.

HOSODA EISHI 1756–1829

114 *Matsukaze* ('The Wind in the Pines')
Published by Izumiya Ichibei
c. 1792
Woodblock (triptych print), 367 × 250 mm (each)
1907.5-31.436

One of ten remaining from a set of 'Genji in
Modern Dress', based on chapters of the
classic novel *Genji Monogatari* ('The Tale of
Genji'), originally written *c.* AD 1000. Here
the Prince visits the mountain retreat of the
Akashi Princess to take away their daughter.
In this way Eishi, born into a samurai family,
introduces the Edo public to his version of
'courtly' style. The print is signed 'Painted by
Eishi'.

HOSODA EISHI

115 *Asagao* ('Morning Glory')
Published by Izumiya Ichibei
c. 1791
Woodblock (triptych print), 372 × 250 mm (each)
1907.5-31.435

Another of the ten designs remaining from
the set 'Genji in Modern Dress', based on
chapters of Murasaki Shikibu's classic novel
of about AD 1000, *Genji Monogatari* ('The Tale
of Genji'). Here the Prince is seen at the
centre indulging in an exchange of poems
with the Lady Asagao. The flower whose
name she bears grows at the left. Eishi uses
the restrained *benigirai* ('hating red') palette
in this series. The print is signed 'Painted by
Eishi'.

114

115

HOSODA EISHI

116 *Tales of Ise*

Published by Nishimuraya Yohachi
c. 1792
Woodblock with applied metal dust (triptych print),
370 × 250 mm (each)
1907.5-31.434

The courtly classic *Ise Monogatari* ('Tales of Ise') is a collection of episodes each explaining the origin
of a poem. It was known to every Japanese with claims to education. Here Eishi links three of the
episodes with a continuous background; the poems are printed in 'courtly' style over a surface
of gold clouds, done here with metal dust. The episodes are, from right to left, nos 27, 1 and 10.
All are depicted in contemporary dress. The signature is 'Painted by Eishi'.

HOSODA EISHI

117 *The courtesan Wakana reading*
Published by Nishimuraya Yōhachi
1794–5
Woodblock, 386 × 264 mm
1945.11-1.024

This is from a series 'The Six Poetic Beauties of the Green Houses', the great brothels of the Shin Yoshiwara licensed district in Edo. The series is very loosely based on the six greatest poets of the ninth century. Here we see Wakana of the Matsubaya House sitting and reading from a poetic anthology. The signature is 'Picture by Eishi'.

HOSODA EISHI

118 *The courtesan Takikawa*
1796–7
Woodblock (one a triptych), 355 × 250 mm
1906.12-20.275

From a three-print set entitled 'A Selection from the Beauties of the Green Houses' (that is, the brothels of the Shin Yoshiwara licensed district). Takikawa was from the Ogiya House, described here as ready for the New Year customers. This sheet is unsigned.

119

120

HOSODA EISHI

119 *The courtesan Nakagawa with two apprentices*
Published by Nishimuraya Yohachi
c. 1795
Woodblock, 385 × 255 mm
1937.7-10.052

The statuesque Nakagawa shows in Eishi's portrayal the
most extreme elongation of all *Ukiyoe* figures, the body
eight times the head, which is further extended by the
high hair-style. As if to emphasise the length, the two
apprentices study a lengthy love-letter to their mistress.
The print's title-cartouche refers to the new premises just
opened by Nakagawa's House of Matsubaya. The
signature is 'Painted by Eishi for fun'.

HOSODA EISHI

120 *A poem by Kisen Hōshi*
Published by Nishimuraya Yohachi
1795–1800
Woodblock, 375 × 243 mm
1927.5-18.05

The series title is 'The Abbreviated Six Poets', on the
lower of the poem cards (top left). On the upper one is a
portrait of Kisen Hōshi and his poem. The prostitute is
holding painted shells for the *kai-awase* game in which
poems are matched up in pairs with their illustrations.
These too refer to the ninth-century poet Kisen, whose
work would be known by every educated Japanese. The
signature is 'Picture by Eishi'.

121

HOSODA EISHŌ
Worked 1793–9

121 *After the bath*
Published by Yamaguchiya Chūsuke
1795–9
Woodblock (pillar print), 617 × 117 mm
1907.5-31.441

A summer scene by Eishi's major
pupil. The woman below is cutting
her nails. The print is signed
'Painted by Eishō'.

HOSODA EISUI
Worked 1797–1804

122 *The Tanabata Festival*
Published by Maruya Bun'emon
c. 1797–1800
Woodblock, 370 × 259 mm
1929.6-11.08

This portrait of the prostitute Tsukasa of the
House of Ōgiya is from a series 'Beauties of the
Five Festivals', which were the main festivals of
the year. The print is a quite complex allusion to
the Tanabata Festival in July which celebrates the
conjunction of the stars Vega and Aquila,
representing lovers who could meet only this
way. Thus Tsukasa represents Orihime, emerging
from her mosquito net (the Milky Way) to gaze at
the portrait of Hikoboshi painted on her fan. The
signature is 'Painted by Ichirakutei Eisui'.

HOSODA EISHI 1756–1829

123 *Portrait of Utamaro*
1815
Hanging scroll, ink and colours on silk, 330 × 398 mm
1913.5-1.0402

This controversial portrait remains unexplained. It
is signed 'Portrait of Utamaro. Painted by
Chōbunsai Eishi in his 60th year'. Utamaro had
died nine years earlier, so some scholars have
assumed (invalidly) that it must be a portrait of
Utamaro II. The likeness is a hostile but not
impossible one when compared with Utamaro's
own idealised self portraits.

123

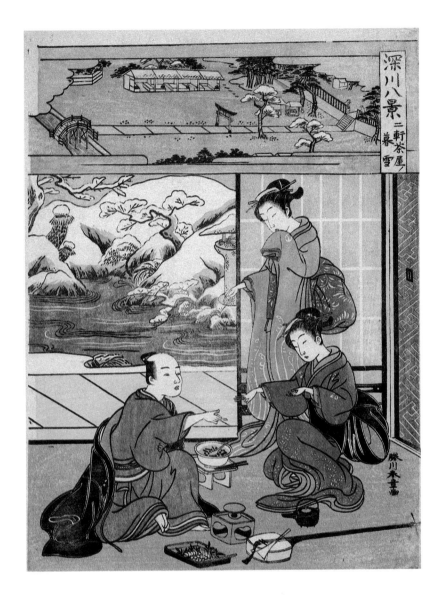

KATSUKAWA SHUNSHŌ 1726–92

124 *Lingering Snow at the Niken Tea-house*

c. 1772
Woodblock, 265 × 199 mm
1926.5-11.010

Two tea-house girls entertain a client in winter.
This is one of a series 'Eight Views of Fukagawa'
showing the riverside district in Edo (Tokyo)
celebrated for its unlicensed brothels. The section
at the top shows the Hachiman shrine where the
tea-house was situated. *Lingering Snow* is one of
the themes of the classical Chinese pictorial set of
'Eight Views of the Xiaoxiang Rivers'. The
signature is 'Painted by Katsukawa Shunshō'.

KATSUKAWA SHUNSHŌ

125 *The actors Matsumoto Kōshirō IV and
Segawa Kikunojō III*

c. 1780
Woodblock, 323 × 225 mm
1945.11-1.012

These were the leading Edo Kabuki players of
their day in female and realistic parts respectively.
Shunshō at this period developed a new and more
vivid style of actor portrait which was only
superseded in 1794 by Sharaku. The signature is
'Painted by Shunshō'.

KATSUKAWA SHUNSHŌ

127 *A View of Enoshima in Sōshū,
       seen from the Direction of Koshigoe*

Published by Tsuruya Kiemon
c. 1780–5
Woodblock, 314 × 452 mm
1906.12-20.145

The island of Enoshima near Kamakura could be reached
by foot at low tide. It has a shrine to Benzaiten, the deity
of wealth and music, and is a favourite place of
pilgrimage. In this rare and early landscape print
Shunshō clearly follows the Europeanised method of
Shiba Kōkan, including the use of shadows. The view is
an artificial one, since Mount Fuji would not be visible
next to Enoshima from this point. The signature is
'Painted by Katsu Shunshō'.

127

KATSUKAWA SHUNSHŌ

126 *Yamauba and a monkey*

Published by Fushimiya Zenroku
?1791–2
Woodblock (one of diptych), 365 × 253 mm
1924.4-30.08

The legendary mountain-witch Yamauba is accompanied by a monkey carrying faggots.
The missing sheet shows her adopted child Kintarō and creatures associated
with him. On the crag Minamoto Yorimitsu seems to be re-enacting his ambush
of the monstrous Shūten Dōji. The print is signed 'Painted by Shunshō'.

KATSUKAWA SHUNCHŌ
Worked *c.* 1781–1801

128 *The Seven Sages in modern dress*
Published by Nishimuraya Yohachi
c. 1788
Woodblock (diptych print), 367 × 242 mm (each)
1910.6-14.11

Shunshō's pupil Shunchō works here in the grander
style popularised by Kiyonaga. A favourite subject for
painting, 'The Seven Chinese Sages of the Bamboo
Grove' is here changed to seven Edo (Tokyo) courtesans
and entertainers, with their attendants. One is reading a
love-letter. The scene is a garden on the outskirts of the
city. The print is signed 'Painted by Shunchō'.

129

130

114

131

KATSUKAWA SHUNCHŌ

129 *A scene from the story of Imoseyama*
Published by Izumiya Ichibei
c. 1788
Woodblock (triptych print), 368 × 242 mm (each)
1909.6-18.33

This is not a Kabuki print as such but it
recreates in contemporary dress a scene from
the popular play *An Example of Noble
Womanhood*. In the play the lovers
Kugonosuke and Hinadori live in palaces
separated by the Yoshino River. Here it is
cherry-blossom time, and Kogonosuke
stands on the far bank gazing at Hinadori,
who stands on the near veranda. The palace
is in the style of a contemporary Edo house
of entertainment. The print is signed
'Painted by Shunchō'.

KATSUKAWA SHUN'EI 1762–1819

130 *A newly published brocade first night*
c. 1795
Woodblock (triptych print), 380 × 250 mm (each)
1927.6-13.018

The scene is outside a Kabuki theatre at a
kaomise (the equivalent of a first night). The
'brocade' of the title refers to the full-colour
printing. A performance can be glimpsed
through the entrance, while two doormen
stand with fans advertising the appearance
of Danjūrō (left) and Sōjūrō. Shun'ei seems
more interested in the beautiful women
passing by. The signature is 'Painted by
Shun'ei'.

KATSUKAWA SHUN'EI

131 *The Tennō Festival*
Published by Yamaguchiya Chūsuke
c. 1795–1800
Woodblock (triptych print), 375 × 255 mm (each)
1910.4-18.181

The Tennō shrine in Edo (Tokyo) had an
ox-headed deity which warded off evil. The
annual festival was in June. A great street
procession outside the shrine centres on two
floats of *shishi* (lion-dogs) carried by bearers.
To the left is a tree covered in devotional
prayer-slips. Such prints have left a vivid and
accurate record of the city of Edo in the
eighteenth and early nineteenth centuries.
The print is signed 'Painted by Shun'ei'.

KATSUKAWA SHUN'EI

132 *The pre-match procession at a Sumō tournament*
Published by Nishimuraya Yohachi
1796
Woodblock (triptych print), 370 × 245 mm (each)
1907.5-31.390

The tournament was held at Kaikōin in October 1796.
The scene is a curious mixture, the recession
well-handled, the wrestlers (admittedly large) shown far
larger than life. The artist depicts the daily *dohyōiri*,
where the senior wrestlers process into the ring in order
of rank, ending with the top-rank *yokozuna*, accompanied
by a sword-bearer. The wrestlers were divided into two
groups – east and west. The wrestler Inazuma shown at
the centre of the ring was the winner of this tournament,
but he failed to reach the upper ranks and retired in 1804.
The signature is 'Painted by Shun'ei'.

133

134

KATSUKAWA SHUNKYOKU
Worked *c.* 1775–95

133 *A Tea-stall Waitress*

c. 1790
Woodblock (pillar print), 693 × 127 mm
1963.7-31.07

The waitress is serving at a tea-stall at the Sansha
Daigongen shrine. The grounds of Shintō shrines and
Buddhist temples were often filled with places of
refreshment. The print is signed 'Painted by Katsukawa
Shunkyoku'.

KATSUKAWA SHUNTEI 1770–1820

134 *The Ōwada Eel Restaurant*

1806
Woodblock (triptych print), 370 × 250 mm (each)
1907.5-31.392

This ambitious print may have been commissioned by
the famous eating-house in Owarimachi to distribute to
favoured customers as souvenirs of their visit.
Restaurants in Japan still often give their customers
mementoes. The elaborate integration of foreground
(staff) and background (customers) is in the style
developed by Toyokuni. The censor's seals are for April
1806, and the signature is 'Painted by Shuntei'.

TŌSHŪSAI SHARAKU
Worked 1794–5

135 *The actor Sanogawa Ichimatsu*
Published by Tsutaya Jūsaburō
1794
Woodblock with powdered mica ground, 380 × 257 mm
1945.11-1.049

The female impersonator plays Shirabito Onayo of Gion, from the play *Hana-ayame Bunroku Soga* ('The Iris Soga Story of the Bunroku Period') performed at the Miyako-za theatre in May 1794. This play was a version of the medieval story of the Soga Brothers' revenge, set here in the late sixteenth century. Sharaku's greatest skill was in catching the personality of the actor under the part, especially in the female roles played by men. The signature is 'Painted by Tōshūsai Sharaku'.

TŌSHŪSAI SHARAKU

136 *The actor Sawamura Sōjūrō as Ōgishi Kurando*
Published by Tsutaya Jūsaburō
1794
Woodblock with powdered mica ground, 360 × 242 mm
1909.6-18.43

From the same play as no. 135. The print is signed 'Painted by Tōshūsai Sharaku'.

TŌSHŪSAI SHARAKU

137 *The actor Bandō Hikosaburo III*
Published by Tsutaya Jūsaburō
1794
Woodblock with powdered mica ground, 358 × 242 mm
1909.6-18.35

Bandō played the role of Sagisaka Sanai in *The Loved Wife's Parti-Coloured Reins*. This play must have made a great impression on the emerging print-designer, for he did nine other portraits from this performance. The signature is 'Painted by Tōshūsai Sharaku'.

TŌSHŪSAI SHARAKU

138 *The actor Ichikawa Ebizō*
Published by Tsutaya Jūsaburō
1794
Woodblock with powdered mica ground, 374 × 245 mm
1945.11-1.042

The play is *The Loved Wife's Parti-Coloured Reins* (see also nos 137, 144–7). The elderly actor had passed on the name of Danjūrō to his successor. He plays here a Nō drama actor who is forced to kill himself because of his daughter's dishonourable liaison. The play was adapted from a Bunraku puppet play, originally by Chikamatsu (1653–1724). The print is signed 'Painted by Tōshūsai Sharaku'.

TŌSHŪSAI SHARAKU

139 *The actor Arashi Ryūzō*
Published by Tsutaya Jūsaburō
1794
Woodblock with powdered mica ground, 355 × 242 mm
1909.6-18.47

From the same play as nos 135 and 136. The role
performed by Ryūzō was Ishibe Kanakichi. The
signature is 'Painted by Tōshūsai Sharaku'.

TŌSHŪSAI SHARAKU

140 *The actor Sakata Hangorō III as Fujikawa
Mizuemon*
Published by Tsutaya Jūsaburō
1794
Woodblock with powdered mica ground, 364 × 240 mm
1909.6-18.36

From the same play as nos 135–6, 139. The print is
signed 'Painted by Tōshūsai Sharaku'.

TŌSHŪSAI SHARAKU

141 *The actor Ichikawa Komazō II as Shiga Daishichi*

Published by Tsutaya Jūsaburō
1794
Woodblock with powdered mica ground, 363 × 242 mm
1909.6-18.48

From the play *Katakiuchi Noriai Banashi* ('A Medley of Tales of Revenge') performed at the Kiri-za theatre, Edo (Tokyo) in 1794. Komazō was celebrated for his high nose, considered suitable for villainous roles. The signature is 'Painted by Tōshūsai Sharaku'.

TŌSHŪSAI SHARAKU

142 *The actors Nakajima Wadaemon and Nakamura Konozō*

Published by Tsutaya Jūsaburō
1794
Woodblock with powdered mica background, 350 × 242 mm
1909.6-18.53

Two minor characters from the same play as no. 141. The characters portrayed are Bodara Chōzaemon and Kanagawaya Gon (a boatman). This is a fine example of Sharaku's interest, unusual among *Ukiyoe* artists, in the more minor players. In some examples of this print the boatman (right) has red make-up across his eyes, apparently applied by hand. The signature is 'Painted by Tōshūsai Sharaku'.

TŌSHŪSAI SHARAKU

143 *The actor Morita Kanya*
Published by Tsutaya Jūsaburō
1794
Woodblock with powdered mica ground, 386 × 252 mm
1906.12-20.202

The part played is Uguisu no Jirosaku, a palanquin
bearer, from a *jōruri* (recited drama) inserted into the
same play as nos 141–2. Kanya is shown twisting his
body in a dance he performed in this episode. The
signature is 'Painted by Tōshūsai Sharaku'.

TŌSHŪSAI SHARAKU

144 *The actor Iwai Hanshirō IV*
Published by Tsutaya Jūsaburō
1794
Woodblock with powdered mica ground, 360 × 235 mm
1909.6-18.46

The celebrated 'moon-faced' female impersonator
in the part of the Nurse in *Koinyobo Somewake
Tazuna* ('The Loved Wife's Parti-Coloured Reins')
performed at the Kawarazaki-za theatre in 1794.
The print is signed 'Painted by Tōshūsai Sharaku'.

TŌSHŪSAI SHARAKU

145 *The female impersonator Osagawa Tsuneyo II*
Published by Tsutaya Jūsaburō
1794
Woodblock with powdered mica ground, 360 × 235 mm
1909.6-18.50

Tsuneyo appeared in May 1794 at the Kawarasaki-za theatre, Edo (Tokyo) in the play *The Loved Wife's Parti-Coloured Reins* (see nos 137–8, 144). Sharaku's 'early' prints, done in the first few months of his shorter than one-year career, make striking use of dark mica backgrounds to bring all the viewer's attention on to the facial expression. The signature is 'Painted by Tōshūsai Sharaku'.

TŌSHŪSAI SHARAKU

146 *The actor Tanimura Torazō*
Published by Tsutaya Jūsaburō
1794
Woodblock with powdered mica ground, 370 × 249 mm
1947.2-13.01

Torazō plays Washizuka Hachiheiji, the villain of the play *The Loved Wife's Parti-Coloured Reins* (see nos 137–8, 144–5). The signature is 'Painted by Tōshūsai Sharaku'.

TŌSHŪSAI SHARAKU

147 *The actor Ōtani Oniji*
Published by Tsutaya Jūsaburō
1794
Woodblock with powdered mica ground, 362 × 244 mm
1909.6-18.41

One of Sharaku's most celebrated portraits, showing
Oniji in the part of the servant Edohei in mid-pose, from
The Loved Wife's Parti-Coloured Reins (see also nos 137–8,
144–6). The signature is 'Painted by Tōshūsai Sharaku'.

TŌSHŪSAI SHARAKU

148 *The actor Yamashita Kinsaku II*
Published by Tsutaya Jūsaburō
1794
Woodblock, 320 × 218 mm
1945.11-1.038

The female impersonator is shown in the role of Iwate
Gozen disguised as Okame, a maid. The play was
Otokoyama Ō-Edo no Ishizue, given at the Kiri-za theatre in
November 1794. In these 'later' prints Sharaku abandons
the mica background and adds a cartouche giving the actors'
alternative names. The signature is 'Painted by Sharaku'.

TŌSHŪSAI SHARAKU

149 *Actors as the lovers Umegawa and Chūbei*

Published by Tsutaya Jūsaburō
1794
Woodblock with powdered mica ground, 360 × 238 mm
1909.6-18.55

The players are Nakayama Tomisaburō as Umegawa and
Ichikawa Komazō II as her feckless lover Chūbei in one
of the many versions of this favourite subject. On this
occasion it was a *jōruri shōsagoto* (recited dance-drama)
given as part of the bill at the Kiri-za theatre in August
1794. The signature is 'Painted by Tōshūsai Sharaku'.

The Late Period

UTAGAWA TOYOHARU
1735–1814

150 *A travesty of the Chinese warrior Kan'u*

c. 1772–81
Woodblock (pillar print), 659 × 114 mm
1908.4-18.1

This print brings together a Japanese scene, a legendary
Chinese hero and European perspective, indicative of
the interest of the eighteenth-century Japanese in the
foreign worlds forbidden to them. In a Shinagawa
brothel (on Edo Bay) a prostitute watches a young client
reading a letter. She holds Kan'u's halberd, in Chinese
legend carried by his retainer. Toyoharu has used an
exaggerated form of perspective to make his print
fashionable. The signature is 'Painted by Toyoharu'.

UTAGAWA TOYOKUNI I 1769–1825

151 Act VI of *Chūshingura*

c. 1790–5
Woodblock (pillar print), 626 × 113 mm
1907.5-31.507

This is a scene from *Chūshingura* ('The Loyal League'),
the most popular of all Kabuki dramas. Kampei, out
shooting boar, notices his father in the distance being
stalked by a robber. The signature is 'Painted by
Toyokuni'.

150

151

UTAGAWA TOYOHARU

152 *A Newly Published Picture of the Chinese Battle at Nine Hermit Mountain*

Published by Iwatoya Gempachi
c. 1781–8
Woodblock, 366 × 510 mm
1963.7-31.06

This elaborate *ukie* ('perspective print') on a Chinese war theme may at first seem far from *Ukiyoe* taste. However, the scene is a realisation of one of the *Bunraku* puppet plays of Chikamatsu Monzaemon (1653–1724), most of which remained very popular through the Edo period. The signature is 'Utagawa Toyoharu Pictured This'.

UTAGAWA TOYOHIRO 1773–1829

153 *The Second Month*

Published by Yamadaya Sanshirō
1801
Woodblock (triptych print), 370 × 235 mm (each)
1909.2-1.312/1924.1-1.01
1924.1-15.04

One of a series entitled 'The Twelve Seasons Painted by Toyohiro and Toyokuni'. These two artists were the most important pupils of Toyoharu. Prostitutes of the Shin Yoshiwara licensed district prepare for the festival of Inari, the fox rice-god. They have made flower-arrangements, prepared offerings, and in the centre are writing a dedicatory inscription. The signature is 'Painted by Toyohiro'.

154

UTAGAWA TOYOKUNI I

154 *The Kachō Tea-house*

Published by Nishimuraya Yohachi
c. 1795–1800
Woodblock (two sheets of a triptych print), 670 × 115 mm
    (each)
1902.2-12.299/300

The left and centre prints of the original three. The
tea-house called Kachō ('Flowers and Birds') became
very popular at this time because of its exotic caged
birds. The hostesses are seen parading with a
young boy who carries birds in cages. The signature is
'Painted by Toyokuni'.

UTAGAWA TOYOKUNI I

155 *A daimyō's lady travelling*

Published by Tsuruya Kinnosuke
c. 1795–1800
Woodblock (triptych print), 383 × 250 mm (each)
1910.4-18.186

A woman from the family of a *daimyō* (feudal lord)
descends from a lacquered *kago* (palanquin). The painted
interior of the *kago* can be glimpsed, and the outside is
decorated with gold leaf and powder. The restrained
colours hint at the aristocratic elegance admired by the
Edo (Tokyo) townspeople. The print is signed 'Painted
by Toyokuni'.

155

156

UTAGAWA TOYOKUNI I

156 *A picnic on the beach*
Published by Tsuruya Kinnosuke
c. 1795–1800
Woodblock (triptych print), 370 × 240 mm (each)
1910.6-14.19

Young men and women of the *daimyō* (feudal
lord) class serve saké from a lacquered picnic
set. In the background fishermen bring in
their catch. Such prints are symbolic of the
gradual mixing of Japan's rigidly defined
classes in the late Edo period. The small red
seal is of the dealer Hayashi who supplied
much of Western Europe with *Ukiyoe* prints,
selling also to Impressionist artists such as
Monet and Van Gogh. The print is signed
'Painted by Toyokuni'.

KIKUGAWA EIZAN 1787–1867

157 *Rosei dreams of Shinagawa*
Published by Yorozuya Kichibei
c. 1820
Woodblock (triptych print), 365 × 255 mm (each)
1909.4-6.473

In a Chinese legend well known in
Edo-period Japan Rosei dreamt of being
Emperor, feasting in the palace and being
carried in procession. Here he dreams of the
pleasures of contemporary Edo (Tokyo). He
greets the sunrise in a boat on Edo Bay,
feasts in a restaurant there, and is
entertained to classical music. He even joins
the procession of a top-rank courtesan as she
parades under the cherry-blossom. The print
is signed 'The brush of Kikugawa Eizan'.

KEISAI EISEN 1791–1848

158 *The grand courtesans Sugatano and
Nanabito with attendants*
Published by Tsutaya Kichizō
c. 1830
Woodblock (triptych print), 365 × 255 mm (each)
1906.12-20.310

A group of prostitutes from the Shin
Yoshiwara licensed district are playing music
on the upper floor of a restaurant
overlooking the Sumida River. Nanabito is
playing the *koto* (a horizontal harp) and
Sugatano the *kokyū* (a single-stringed violin).
They are accompanied by lower-rank
prostitutes and apprentices. With the
introduction of Prussian blue about this time,
some prints were done in the new colour
alone to exploit its novelty. This example also
uses a little red on the lips. The signature is
'Printed by Keisai Eisen'.

157

158

131

159

161

160

KEISAI EISEN

159 *Looking at Mt Asama, the Oiwake stop on the Kisokaidō*
Published by Takeuchi Magohachi (Hōeidō)
Reprint; the original *c*. 1835
Woodblock, 230 × 360 mm
1952.10-11.018

This is a reprint, without his signature, of one of Eisen's twenty-four
prints from this series of seventy-one on the posting-stations along the
inland route between Edo (Tokyo) and Kyoto. Eisen's name was dropped
after a disagreement with the publisher Hōeidō, who also later withdrew
from the series, and Hiroshige completed the other forty-seven subjects.
The poor registration top and bottom indicates a reprint of about 1850–70.

KEISAI EISEN

160 *The souvenir shop at the Narai stop on the Kisokaidō*
Published by Takeuchi Magohachi (Hōeidō)
c. 1835
Woodblock, 246 × 377 mm
1906.12-20.973

From the same series as no. 159. Hōeidō and Hiroshige had established a
gentle landscape style with the Tōkaidō Road series, but Eisen's
contributions have a sharply sensitive quality of their own.
The signature 'Painted by Eisen' is missing in later reprints.

KEISAI EISEN

161 *A distant view of Inagawa Bridge at the Nojiri stop on the Kisokaidō*
Published by Takeuchi Magohachi (Hōeidō)
c. 1835
Woodblock, 248 × 367 mm
1941.2-8.05

A very fine early edition, complete with Eisen's signature which was
dropped for later reprints. The Kannon Hall of the Kiyomizu Temple can be
seen in silhouette (top left). The mixture of Chinese and 'expressionist'
elements shows the influence of Hokusai's 'Thirty-six Views of Fuji' (see no. 172).
The series of views on the Kisokaidō Road was begun by
Eisen and completed by Hiroshige, both artists contributing many
distinguished prints. The signature is 'Painted by Eisen'.

UTAGAWA KUNISADA (TOYOKUNI III)
1786–1864

162 *A sudden summer shower*
Published by Hamadaya Tokubei
1848–52
Woodblock (triptych print), 345 × 255 mm (each)
1907.5-31.608

In Japanese lore lightning never strikes a mulberry field or a mosquito
net. Ordinary country people are seen running for both as the lightning
flashes. The wooden shutters are also being hurriedly put into place.
The printing of mosquito nets was a particular pride of the *Ukiyoe* publishers.
It was done with separate blocks for the vertical and horizontal lines.
The print is signed 'Painted by Kōchōrō Toyokuni' (right), 'Painted by
Ichiyōsai Toyokuni' (centre) and 'Painted by Toyokuni' (left).
Kunisada took the name of Toyokuni in 1844 and
thereafter always used it.

163

UTAGAWA KUNIYOSHI 1797–1861

163 *Notes on women's conduct – stretching fabrics*
Published by Marusei (Maruya Seijirō)
c. 1842
Woodblock (triptych print), 365 × 240 mm (each)
1907.5-31.622

From time to time the authorities decided *Ukiyoe* prints were too frivolous. One such time was in 1842, and the artists temporarily responded by turning their beautiful women into models of the virtues. Here serving-women are washing an *obi* (sash) and stretching it out to dry. The inscription, printed over a repeating textile pattern, observes that this is better than buying new ones. The signatures are 'Painted by Ichiyūsai Kuniyoshi' (right and centre) and 'Painted by Chōōrō Kuniyoshi' (left).

UTAGAWA KUNIYOSHI

164 *Tametomo and his son rescued by the tengu*
Published by Sumiyoshiya Masugorō
1848–52
Woodblock (triptych print), 365 × 250 mm (each)
1906.12-20.1339

This is one of the extravagantly heroic compositions produced by Kuniyoshi in response to the government crack-down on more frivolous subjects. It is based on the novel by Kyokutei Bakin (1767–1848) *Chinsetsu Yumiharizuki* and Hokusai's illustrations to it. Fleeing by sea from defeat in the Heiji Wars, Tametomo's party are overcome by a storm. His wife throws herself into the sea to placate the waves, while Kihei saves their child by climbing on to the back of a huge shark. Tametomo is stopped from killing himself by the spirits of mythical creatures called *tengu*, followers of the dead Emperor Sutoku. The signature is 'Painted by Ichiyūsai Kuniyoshi'.

UTAGAWA KUNIYOSHI

165 *The ghosts of the Heike*
Published by Enshuya Hikobei
1848–52
Woodblock (triptych print), 365 × 250 mm (each)
1907.5-31.230

This heroic subject is based on the Nō drama piece *Funa Benkei* ('Benkei in the Boat'). The Minamoto clan hero Yoshitsune and his men are on a ship, when they are attacked by the ghosts of the Heike who were drowned at the Battle of Dannoura. Yoshitsune's retainer, the gigantic Benkei, repulses them with his presence and courage. Benkei is seen on the stern of the ship. The signature is 'Painted by Ichiyūsai Kuniyoshi'.

164

165

166

KATSUSHIKA HOKUSAI 1760–1849

166 *Tametomo and the bow*

1811

Hanging scroll, ink, colour and gold on silk, 593 × 819 mm

1881.12-20.1747

This important documentary painting commemorates the publication of the book *Chinsetsu Yumiharizuki* by the novelist Kyokutei Bakin (1767–1848) with illustrations by Hokusai. It refers to the 'bow-stretching' of the book's punning title. The hero Tametomo challenges the wild inhabitants of Onoshima Island to test their strength against him. The inscription dated equivalent to AD 1811 is by Bakin himself. The painting is signed 'Painted by Katsushika Hokusai Taitō' and is sealed 'Raishin'.

KATSUSHIKA HOKUSAI

167 *A seller of fortune-telling poems*

1827

Hanging scroll, ink and light colours on paper, 1240 × 503 mm

1913.5-1.0317

The poems are written on *tanzaku* (poem-slips) and tied to a bow. Recent research has suggested that this is a portrait of the playwright Kanze Motomasa. However, the facial likeness is very close to Hokusai's portraits of himself. The signature is 'Respectfully painted by Hokusai I-itsu', and the date is Bunsei 10 (= 1827), first month.

KATSUSHIKA HOKUSAI 1760–1849

168 *Ducks in the water*

1847

Hanging scroll, ink and colours on silk, 1113 × 403 mm

1913.5-1.0320

A fine example of Hokusai's evergreen skill in his last years. The signature is 'Eighty-eight year-old Manji'.

136

167

168

137

KATSUSHIKA HOKUSAI

169 *Chūnagon Kanesuke's poem*

c. 1840

Ink sketch on paper (fair copy for a print), 248 × 366 mm
1905.6-8.1

This *hanshitae*, or final outline copy prepared for
cutting the block for printing, is for a print series
called 'The Hundred Poems by a Hundred Poets
Explained in Pictures by the Nurse', of which
twenty-seven were actually printed. One was
prepared for printing, while sixty-eight drawings
remain unprinted, only four designs of the 100
being unaccounted for. Each design popularises
one of the classical thirteenth-century anthology
Ōgura Hyakunin Isshū. Kanesuke's poem refers to
his yearning for his beloved by the Izumi River.
The sketch is signed 'Manji, formerly Hokusai'.

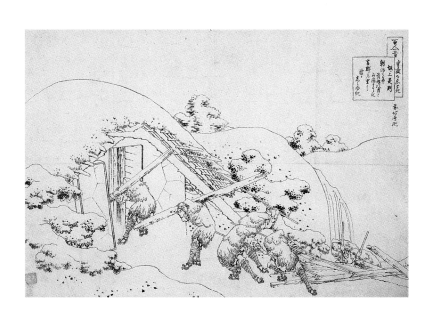

KATSUSHIKA HOKUSAI

170 *Sakanoue Korenori's poem*

c. 1840
Ink sketch on paper (fair copy for a print), 252 × 367 mm
1913.5-1.0345

Another unprinted *hanshitae* for the print series
'The Hundred Poems by a Hundred Poets
Explained in Pictures by the Nurse'. It illustrates
Korenori's famous poem on the subject of the
snow falling at Yoshino in the dawn moonlight.
Carpenters are building, or rebuilding, a
mountain hut. The sketch is signed 'Manji,
formerly Hokusai'.

KATSUSHIKA HOKUSAI

171 *The poem of Kōka Mon'in no Bettō*

c. 1840
Ink sketch on paper (fair copy for a print), 250 × 371 mm
1937.7-10.0286

Another unprinted *hanshitae* for the print series
'The Hundred Poems by a Hundred Poets
Explained in Pictures by the Nurse'. It illustrates a
poem by the lady sometimes known as the
Daughter of Toshikata, in which she yearns for
her love by the reeds of the Naniwa River. In
Hokusai's design reeds (perhaps for thatching)
are being transported on a two-wheeled cart. The
sketch is signed, 'Manji, formerly Hokusai'.

KATSUSHIKA HOKUSAI

172 *A favourable breeze and clear weather*
Published by Nishimuraya Yohachi
c. 1830
Woodblock, 261 × 382 mm
1906.12-20.525

One of the greatest images from Hokusai's monumental series 'Thirty-six Views of Mount Fuji', in which he used Prussian blue extensively for the first time in the history of the Japanese print and established landscape as a major new print genre. This design is often known in English as 'Fuji in Clear Weather' and in Japan as Akafuji ('Red Fuji'). The signature is 'The brush of Hokusai, changing his name to I-itsu'.

KATSUSHIKA HOKUSAI

173 *The Tonegawa River in Shimōsa Province*
Published by Moriya Jihei
c. 1830
Woodblock, 171 × 257 mm
1930.11-12.05

A rare print from the series *Chie no Umi* ('The Sea in a Thousand Pictures'). The series in fact consists of only ten prints. The signature is 'Formerly Hokusai, changing his name to I-itsu'.

KATSUSHIKA HOKUSAI

174 *The carp and the waterfall*
Published by Moriya Jihei
c. 1830–5
Woodblock, 520 × 230 mm
1927.4-13.014

This is a *kakemonoe*, or print in the form of a hanging scroll. The Chinese legend was that carp which could ascend the Yellow River falls would turn into dragons. In Japan the ascending carp became a symbol of courage and was used especially for Boys' Day (5 May). This print is in Hokusai's 'Chinese' style. The signature is 'Formerly Hokusai, changing his name to I-itsu'.

175

176

KATSUSHIKA HOKUSAI

175 *The horsetail gatherer*

Published by Moriya Jihei
c. 1840
Woodblock, 500 × 230 mm
1910.4-18.194

This is from a series of ten prints, in hanging-scroll
format, entitled 'A Realistic Mirror of Poets' (or 'Poetry' –
the title is punning), based on well-known Chinese and
Japanese poems. This subject is based on the Nō drama
Tokusa Kari, where an old reed-gatherer seeks and finds
his lost child in the mountains of Shinanō. The Nō chant
refers to the autumn moon emerging from the trees on
Mount Sonohara. The signature is 'The brush of the
former Hokusai, changing his name to I-itsu'.

KATSUSHIKA HOKUSAI

176 *Youthful progress*

Published by Moriya Jihei
c. 1840
Woodblock, 500 × 226 mm
1906.12-20.571

Another print from the series of ten entitled 'A Realistic
Mirror of Poets', based on well-known Chinese and
Japanese poems. In several of this series Hokusai
favoured a combination of the new Prussian blue and the
old red vegetable dye *beni*. The subject here is based on
the story of the Han Period Chinese poet Cui Guofu who
lost his whip in the capital of Changan and used a
willow-branch instead. The signature is 'The brush of the
former Hokusai, changing his name to I-itsu'.

KATSUSHIKA HOKUSAI

177 Three *tanzaku* (poem-slips)

Published by Moriya Jihei
c. 1825
Woodblock, 350 × 68 mm (each approx.)
1928.11-26.08(1-3)

Long, thin slips for writing poems on were called *tanzaku*
and were often decorated, but it is doubtful that these
printed versions were intended to write over. They
show, from left to right, 'Sweeping maple-leaves',
'Washing cloth' and 'Pilgrims writing on a pillar'. The
first two are signed 'The brush of the former Hokusai,
changing his name to I-itsu', and the third is signed
'Painted by the former Hokusai'.

177

TOTOYA HOKKEI 1780–1850

178 *Mother and child*

c. 1835
Hanging scroll, ink and colours on silk, 552 × 1073 mm
1881.12-20.1906

Hokkei was Hokusai's most skilled pupil and in
brushwork if not in imagination the equal of his
master. The woman, almost certainly a courtesan,
has been taken by surprise by her son's
behaviour, and has dropped her paper napkins (a
traditional symbol of passion in *Ukiyoe*). He is
tracing the syllable *no* in the mist of the metal
mirror. We are left to guess why it should be
misted. The bowl beside him holds
cherry-blossoms. The signature is 'Aoigaoka
Hokkei' and the seal is 'Kyōsai'.

ANDŌ HIROSHIGE 1797–1858

179 *Evening Moon at the Ryōgoku Bridge*
Published by Kawaguchiya Shōzō
c. 1830
Woodblock, 242 × 365 mm
1955.4-16.05

This dramatically composed piece is from Hiroshige's first major landscape series 'Tōto Meisho' ('Famous Spots in the Eastern City'), which consisted of ten prints. They established him as a rival to Hokusai in the landscape form. Through the beams of the Ryōgoku Bridge at Asakusa in Edo (Tokyo) can be seen the Fukagawa district, with Hitotsubashi (a smaller bridge) and the angled roofs of the government boat-houses. The signature is 'Painted by Ichiyūsai Hiroshige'.

ANDŌ HIROSHIGE

180 *Geese at Haneda*
Published by Sanoya Kihei
c. 1837
Woodblock, 258 × 367 mm
1938.3-12.011

One of the series 'Edo Kinkō Hakkei no Uchi' ('From Eight Views in the Environs of Edo' = Tokyo). The series was originally commissioned by the comic-verse poet Taihaidō Donshō and includes his poems printed in the sky. These were reduced in later printings. The scene is the Benten shrine at Haneda. The descending geese, one of the classic eight subjects for a landscape set, are curiously appropriate for the district, now Tokyo's domestic airport. The signature is 'Painted by Hiroshige'.

ANDŌ HIROSHIGE

181 *Night Rain at Karasaki*
Jointly published by Takeuchi Magohachi (Hōeidō) and
    Yamamotoya Heikichi (Eikyūdō)
c. 1835
Woodblock, 253 × 379 mm
1907.5-31.586

From the series 'Eight Views of Lake Biwa', which
has some claim to be Hiroshige's masterpiece in
pure landscape. In this version the printing is
done in ink and blue only, and the rain seems to
fall in cold weather on the celebrated pine-tree,
which was so large that its boughs had to be
supported on stakes. The cartouche (top left)
reproduces a well-known poem on the scene. The
print is signed 'Painted by Hiroshige'.

ANDŌ HIROSHIGE

182 *Night Rain at Karasaki*
Jointly published by Takeuchi Magohachi (Hōeidō) and
    Yamamotoya Heikichi (Eikyūdō)
c. 1835
Woodblock, 248 × 368 mm
1941.2-8.04

In this version the feeling of the print is
transformed by the use of green on the block for
the pine-tree. The season now seems to be May or
June. This set of 'Eight Views of Lake Biwa' is
based on a series of subjects used in Japanese art
since the Muromachi Period (1392–1573) and in
turn based on the classic Chinese series 'Eight
Views of the Xiaoxiang Rivers'. The signature is
'Painted by Hiroshige'.

ANDŌ HIROSHIGE

183 *Crossing the Yoroi Waterway*

Published by Kawaguchiya Shōzō
c. 1837
Woodblock, 238 × 365 mm
1906.12-20.879

From the series 'Kōto Shōkei' ('Splendid Views of
the River Capital'). As Hiroshige's success in
views of Edo (Tokyo) increased, his publishers
had to find new titles for series which were
substantially on the same theme. This print shows
ferries and freight-boats (one loaded with
saké-casks) on a tributary waterway to the Sumida
River. The crossing is between Kayabachō and
Koamichō. A fire-watching tower is prominent in
the background, reminding us that Hiroshige was
a hereditary fire official. The print is signed
'Painted by Hiroshige'.

ANDŌ HIROSHIGE

184 *Seba*

Published by Iseya Toshibei
c. 1840
Woodblock, 244 × 368 mm
1906.12-20.933

Considered by many to be the artist's masterpiece
in the medium, this print is from the Kisokaidō
Road series begun by Eisen (see also nos 159–61)
and completed by Hiroshige with a new
publisher, who changed the title to 'From the
sixty-nine Posting Stations on the Kisokaidō Road'
(there are actually seventy-one in the series). Seba
is in reality surrounded by mountains, and the
Narai River is far narrower there than in the print.
It is thus virtually an imaginary moonlit
landscape. The signature is 'Painted by
Hiroshige'.

185

ANDŌ HIROSHIGE

185 *Mountain River on the Kiso Road*
Published by Okazawaya Taheiji
1857
Woodblock (triptych print), 365 × 245 mm (each)
1910.4-18.197

One of the three great triptychs made in Hiroshige's last year on the traditional set of 'Snow, Moon and Flowers'. In these works the artist finally placed himself, through the print medium he understood best, in the great landscape tradition of East Asia. In this example especially he recaptures some of that grandeur, in which human figures are so tiny that they seem there only to emphasise the scale of the natural world. The signature is 'The brush of Hiroshige'.

ANDŌ HIROSHIGE

186 *A night view of the eight great places of Buyō Kanazawa*
Published by Okazawaya Taheiji
1857
Woodblock (triptych print), 365 × 245 mm (each)
1910.4-18.196

This is the 'Moon' section of the 'Snow, Moon and Flowers' set done by Hiroshige in his last year, apparently as a summing-up of his achievements in landscape. These three compositions are certainly the grandest of all Japanese landscape prints. The eight famous places of Kanazawa (now in Kanagawa Prefecture) have been obliterated by filling-in of the coast. The signature is 'The brush of Hiroshige'.

ANDŌ HIROSHIGE

187 *View of Awa no Narutō*
Published by Okazawaya Taheiji
1857
Woodblock (triptych print), 370 × 250 mm (each)
1908.7-14.50

This is the third of the set of triptychs on the 'Snow, Moon and Flowers' theme done by Hiroshige in his last year. The 'flowers' are the foam of the whirlpool rapids at Narutō in Awa, between the islands of Awaji and Shikoku. The latter is in the distance. The signature is 'The brush of Hiroshige'.

186

187

Surimono

KUBOTA SHUMMAN 1757–1820

188 *Gathering spring flowers*

c. 1800
Woodblock (*surimono* print), 185 × 518 mm
1927.10-13.03

The servants of an upper-class woman gather flowers. The signature is 'Painted by Shōsadō Kubo Shumman'.

KUBOTA SHUMMAN

189 *Descending geese in autumn*

c. 1800
Woodblock with blind-printing and applied metal dust
 (*surimono* print), 205 × 554 mm
1907.5-31.429

The moon, the descending geese and the bush-clover are all symbols of autumn. The space left on this composition implies it was to be written on. It originally also had a folded-over blank sheet at the bottom. The seal reads 'Shumman'.

188

189

190

191

KATSUKAWA SHUN'EI 1762–1819

190 *Congratulations on new names*

c. 1790–1800
Woodblock (*surimono* print), 189 × 503 mm
1924.3-27.012

This print was issued for Boys' Day (5 May) as shown by the deflated paper carp to the left and the two heroes represented. One is the legendary Chinese hero Shoki, 'the Demon Queller', who is is shown on a half-unrolled hanging scroll. The other is the Japanese Yanone no Gorō, as acted by Ichikawa Danjūrō, but in the form of a doll. The two celebrities who had received new names (a form of promotion) were the actor Ichikawa Hakuen and the writer Danshūrō Emba. The print is signed (on the scroll) 'Painted by Shun'ei'.

KATSUSHIKA HOKUSAI 1760–1849

191 *Cherry-viewing on a balcony*

1797–8
Woodblock (*surimono* print), 139 × 580 mm
1919.6-1.01

The left-hand side is filled with recent *kyōka* (comic poems) by a poetry club, by whom the print must have been commissioned. The print is signed 'Painted by Hokusai Sōri'.

KATSUSHIKA HOKUSAI

192 *A woman washing*

1799
Woodblock (*surimono* print), 200 × 525 mm
1906.12-20.473

A woman is about to wash her face from the ritual lacquered basin called a *tsunodarai*. The inscription makes it clear that this is an advertisement for a *jōruri* (recited drama) performance on the 23rd of the sixth month. The signature is 'Painted by Sōri changing his name to Hokusai'.

KATSUSHIKA HOKUSAI

193 *The Wistaria Arbour*

c. 1801–7
Woodblock (*surimono* print), 188 × 514 mm
1924.3-27.018

A lady of the *daimyō* (feudal lord) class sits on her veranda and looks at the wistaria in blossom. The print is signed 'The Old Man Mad About Painting, Hokusai'.

KATSUSHIKA HOKUSAI

194 *Princess Jōruri and Yoshitsune*

c. 1801–7
Woodblock (*surimono* print), 189 × 514 mm
1920.5-14.09

The princess, having attracted Yoshitsune by her *koto* playing, is in turn entranced by his flute. She has sent her maid to the gate to find out who it is. The resulting love affair ends in her suicide. The signature is 'Painted by Hokusai, the Old Man Mad About Painting'.

KATSUSHIKA HOKUSAI

195 *Going to the East*

c. 1803–6
Woodblock (*surimono* print),
425 × 575 mm
1907.5-31.576

This is a travesty of the story of the poet Ariwara no Narihira, told in the *Ise Monogatari* ('Tales of Ise'). Exiled from the Court at Kyoto and sent to the east, he paused on his journey to admire Mount Fuji. Here the poet and attendants are all women. The pine-tree and the mountain are New Year symbols. The print is signed 'Painted by Katsushika Hokusai'.

KATSUSHIKA HOKUSAI

196 *Cherry-trees in blossom in the mist*

c. 1810
Woodblock with blind-printing (*surimono* print), 392 × 545 mm
1907.5-31.578

The print originally had a blank sheet attached to it for greetings. The signature has been trimmed, and only 'Hokusai' is visible.

KATSUSHIKA HOKUSAI

197 *Tametomo and two salt-gatherers*

c. 1808
Woodblock (*surimono* print),
189 × 515 mm
1937.7-10.0217

This print seems to be an advertisement for *Chinsetsu Yumiharitsuki* by Takizawa Bakin (1767–1848) with illustrations by Hokusai. Tametomo's bow is the 'Yumi' of the punning title. The printed inscription is by Bakin and refers to the book and to the play developed from it. The signature is 'Painted by Katsushika Hokusai Tōka'.

199

200

TOTOYA HOKKEI 1770–1850

198 *Scenes from the childhood of Kintarō*

c. 1830
Woodblock with applied metal dust (two-sheet *surimono* print),
    418 × 360 mm
1922.2-13.02

This extraordinary display of printing technique seems
to be the work of a Kyoto or Osaka publisher. The
legendary Red Boy of the mountains is shaking a tree
down to make a bridge over a torrent. Creatures called
tengu fall out of it, one holding a board marked
'nightingale'. By the tree sits his mother Yaegiri,
sometimes known as Yamauba. Yorimitsu (top right)
arrives to discover the boy and adopt him. Two poems
are showered with cherry-blossoms. The allusions of this
complex print are not all explained. The signature is
'Painted by Hokkei'.

YASHIMA GAKUTEI ?1786–1868

199 *The Taketori Princess returns to heaven*

c. 1830
Woodblock with blind printing and applied gold and silver dust
    (four-sheet *surimono* print), 207 × 182 mm (each)
1941.2-8.010

A rare and sumptuous *surimono* composition in four
sheets. The scene is the end of one of the best-known
Japanese fairy-tales. The little child found in a bamboo
stump by the old bamboo-cutter grows up under his care
and is finally revealed as a princess from heaven, to
which she returns in a splendid procession. Each sheet is
printed with appropriate thirty-one syllable poems. The
signature is 'Gakutei' and the seal 'Sadaoka'.

UTAGAWA KUNIHIRO
Worked *c.* 1815–43

200 *Formal portrait of the actor Arashi Kichisaburō II*
?1820
Woodblock with applied lacquer and mother-of-pearl
    (*surimono* print), 377 × 505 mm
1906.12-20.1131

Kichisaburō was one of the most popular actors of his
day, and like many of his colleagues was a *haiku* poet as
well. This print probably celebrates his change of name
in 1820 to Kitsusaburō. To the right are printed a series of
congratulatory *haiku* by his friends, with his own at the
bottom, signed with a pen-name Rikan. He is shown in
formal attire with a sword-bearer, a status much coveted
by those not of samurai origin. His elbow-rest is printed
with lacquer and mother-of-pearl, a rare, costly and
difficult process. The signature is 'Copied by Kunihiro'.

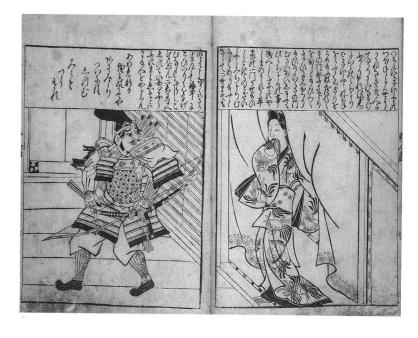

HISHIKAWA MORONOBU *c.* 1618–94

1 *Ukiyo Hyakunin Onna* ('One Hundred
    Women of the Floating World')

Illustrated: Court ladies preparing for a moon-viewing
    party
Published by Kashiwaya Yoichi
1 vol., 1681
Woodblock, 260 × 190 mm
Hillier 30

With its sumptuous idealisations of women of all
classes, this is one of the early masterpieces of
Ukiyoe art in graphic form.

HISHIKAWA MORONOBU

2 *(Shimpan) Bijin Ezukushi*
    ('A (Newly Published) Series of Pictures
    of Beautiful Women')

Illustrated: The medieval warrior Taira No Michimori
    takes leave of a courtesan (who is dressed in
    17th-century style)
Published by Urokogataya
3 vols, 1683
Woodblock, 273 × 185 mm
Hillier 32

FURUYAMA MOROSHIGE
Worked *c.* 1678–98

3 *Kōshoku Edo Murasaki*
   ('The Sensual "Violets" of Edo')

Illustrated: Otsune Kuduko (standing) and Gen no Mōke
   reading a letter
A brief colophon quotes 'A publisher in Tōri abura-chō'
   (in Edo)
1 vol., *c.* 1686
Woodblock, 223 × 156 mm
Hillier 41

An illustrated edition of an erotic novel by
Ishikawa Ryūsen, typical in style and content of
the expansive late seventeenth-century society of
Edo, Kyoto and Osaka.

SUGIMURA JIHEI
Worked 1680–1704

4 *Yamato Fūryū Ekagami*
   ('Japan Mirrored in Elegant Pictures')

Illustrated: Fashionable townsmen with entertaining-
   women on a country excursion
Published by Yamagataya Ichirōemon, probably Edo
1 vol., 1684
Woodblock, with 19th-century hand-colouring, 250 × 188 mm
Hillier 35

The finest of Sugimura's non-erotic books, its
black and white brilliance unhappily lessened by
crude hand-colouring of a much later date. One
other copy is known, in the Museum of Fine Arts,
Boston. It is in scroll form with a similar
manuscript title. Like this copy it is incomplete,
but the two together appear to make a complete
book, less any preface there may have been.

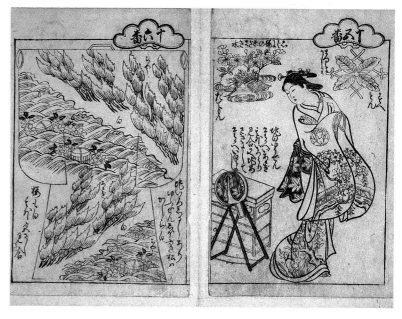

YOSHIDA HAMBEI
Worked *c.* 1664–89

5 *Nihon Etai-gura*
   ('Japan's Treasury for the Ages')

Illustrated: Fudōya and the beggars from Saikaku's novel
   Nihon Etai Gura (book 4)
Published by Kaneya, Kyoto, and Morita Shōtarō, Osaka
2 vols, 1688
Woodblock, 265 × 180 mm
Hillier 45

This is the first edition of one of the best known of
Saikaku's *ukiyo-zōshi* ('novels of the Floating
World'), frequently reprinted in modern times.
Although unsigned, the illustrations are typical
Hambei. Saikaku was the best-known novelist of
the Edo period.

NISHIKAWA SUKENOBU 1671–1750

6 *Chinsoku Hinagata Miyako Fuzoku*
   ('Rare and Popular Kimono Patterns
   of the Capital')

Illustrated: Kimono pattern (left) and woman looking in a
   mirror (right)
Published by Kobayashi Kiemon, Nishimura Riemon and
   Tanimura Seibei, Kyoto
1 vol., 1716
Woodblock, 243 × 165 mm
Hillier 64

The kimono designs are interspersed with
full-length figures of girls and *wakashū*
(fashionable young men) in the latest styles.

NISHIKAWA SUKENOBU

7 *Hyakunin Jorō Shinasadame* ('Critical
  Studies of One Hundred Women')

Illustrated: A madam, with her girls
Published by Hachimonjiya Hachizaemon, Kyoto
2 vols, 1723
Woodblock, 285 × 195 mm
Hillier 70

Volume 1 portrays women of all vocations and
classes; volume 2 courtesans of high and low
degree. This is one of the masterpieces of *Ukiyoe*
art and of the black and white style.

NISHIKAWA SUKENOBU

8 *Ehon Asakayama*
  ('Picture-book of Mount Asaka')

Illustrated: Courtesan with baby boy (left) and courtesan
  with kitten and apprentice (right)
Published by Kikuya Kihei, Kyoto
1 vol., 1739
Woodblock, 260 × 180 mm
Hillier 80

Despite the title, this is another book of pictures of
beautiful women and represents Sukenobu's art at
its most charming. The connection of the
beauty-spot of Mount Asaka with the subject of
the book is uncertain. Two editions are known,
both with the same date, one (thought to be the
later) prefaced by three double-page designs
which are lacking in this copy.

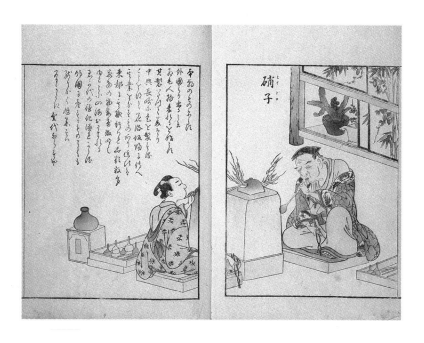

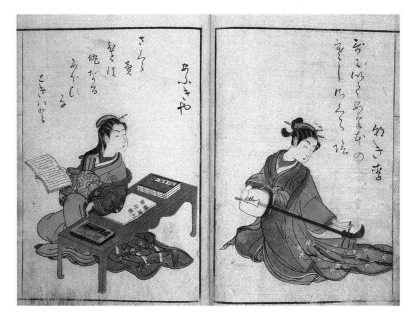

TACHIBANA MINKŌ
Worked 1760s–70s

9 *Saiga Shokunin Burui* ('Various Classes of
Artisans in Coloured Pictures')

Illustrated: Glass-blower
Published by Nemura Tōsaburō and Sawa Isuke
2 vols, 1770
Stencil printed, 285 × 190 mm
Hillier 118

Probably the finest *kappazuri* (stencil) work ever
produced in Japan and a deeply interesting
account of contemporary craftsmanship.
Illustrated is a rare picture of glass-blowing, a
little-known craft in Edo Japan.

SUZUKI HARUNOBU 1724–70

10 *Ehon Seirō Bijin Awase*
('Picture-book Bringing Together the
Beauties of the Green Houses')

Illustrated: The courtesans Tokiwado (left), reading *The
Tale of Genji*, and Asagiri (right), playing the *samisen*
Published by Maruya Jimpachi, Koizumi Chūgōrō and
Funaki Kanosuke
5 vols, 1770
Woodblock, 266 × 165 mm
OA 58

Courtesans of the great houses (the 'Green
Houses') are portrayed in Harunobu's most
extensive work, and one of the earliest
masterpieces of the full colour-printed woodblock
book in Japan. The work is also a treasury of detail
on the textiles and applied arts of the day.

KATSUKAWA SHUNSHŌ 1726–92
KITAO SHIGEMASA 1739–1820
UTAGAWA TOYOHARU 1735–1814

11 *Jūnikō* ('The Twelve Seasons')

Illustrated: (left) Shunshō, The Seventh Month – the
   Tanabata Festival; (right) Toyoharu, The Sixth Month –
   the Gion Festival
Published by Urokogataya Magobei
1 vol., *c.* 1770
Folding album, woodblock, 248 × 185 mm
OA 72

This is an album made up of a series of twelve
sheet-prints, of which this is apparently the only
complete set, perhaps issued in album form
slightly later. The title is an informal one and does
not appear on the prints, each of which has as its
title the name of a festival celebrated in that
month. Each composition is divided into two
different aspects of the festival.

KITAO SHIGEMASA
KATSUKAWA SHUNSHŌ

12 *Seirō Bijin Awase Sugata Kagami* ('A Mirror of Beautiful Women of the Green Houses Compared')

Illustrated: Courtesans of the Shinkanaya House writing,
   reading and tying poem-slips to bamboo
Published by Yamazaki Kimbei and Tsutaya Jūsaburō
3 vols, 1776
Woodblock, 280 × 185 mm
Hillier 124

Acknowledged as one of the outstanding
illustrated books of the world. The 'Green
Houses' were the great establishments of
courtesans in Edo. The seasons are represented by
flowers at the beginning of each volume – spring
and summer in volume 1, autumn and winter in
volume 2. Volume 3 has verses on the four
seasons written by the courtesans depicted in the
prints.

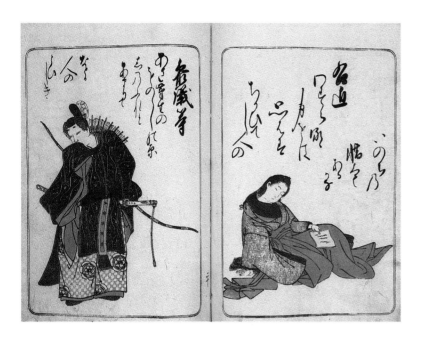

KATSUKAWA SHUNSHŌ

13 *Nishiki Hyakunin Isshu Azuma Ori*
    ('The Hundred Poets Brocaded in the
    Eastern Weave')

Illustrated: The classic poets Sangi Hitoshi (left) and Ukon
    (right)
Published by Kariganeya Seikichi and Kariganeya
    Ginosuke
1 vol., 1775
Woodblock, 280 × 182 mm
OA 110

This is a version of the anthology of *Hyakunin
Isshū* ('One Hundred Poems by One Hundred
Poets'), originally collected in the thirteenth
century. The 'Brocade' of the title refers to the
newly popular full-colour prints known as *nishikie*
and the 'Eastern Weave' refers to the style of Edo
(Tokyo), the 'Eastern capital'. The introductory
pages are in pure *Ukiyoe* style.

KATSUKAWA SHUNSHŌ
IPPITSUSAI BUNCHŌ
Worked *c.* 1756–95

14 *Ehon Butai Ōgi* ('Picture-book
    of the Stage in Fan-shapes')

Illustrated: Bunchō, the Kabuki actors Azuma Tōzō as
    Sonoe (left) and Ichikawa Benzō as Umimara
Published by Kariganeya Ihei
3 vols, 1770
Woodblock, 268 × 177 mm
OA 118

This is one of the most comprehensive collections
of actor-portraits of the period by the two leading
artists of the day in this field. The pale blue
backgrounds have faded to beige on every sheet.

TORIYAMA SEKIEN 1712–88

15 *Sekien Gafu* ('Sekien's Picture-album')
Illustrated: Women of Ōhara
Published by Enshūya Yashichi and Yūrien Tōshū
2 vols, 1774
Woodblock, 318 × 215 mm
Hillier 478

Sekien was Utamaro's teacher. Here he runs the gamut from Kanō landscape to *Ukiyoe*, and the print-makers give a virtuoso interpretation from the extremely delicate to the vigorously bold.

ISODA KORYŪSAI
Worked *c.* 1766–88

16 *Azuma Nishiki Matsu-no-kurai*
    ('Courtesans in Brocades of the East')
Illustrated: Courtesans of the House of Tamaya watching
   a dance
Published by Urokagataya Magobei
1 vol., preface dated 1777
Woodblock, 218 × 162 mm
Hillier 129

The title needs some explanation: 'Brocades of the East' was a way of describing Edo (Azuma, or East) colour prints. According to tradition, the title *Matsu-no-kurai* ('The High Steward of the Pine') was conferred by the first Chin Emperor of China on a pine-tree under which he sheltered during a rainstorm. In the Edo period it was one of the numerous nicknames for courtesans. This is a book of exceptional rarity (no complete copy is known) owing to the fact that all seem to have been divided up. Single pages are fairly common.

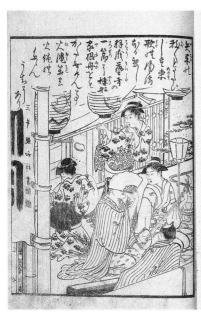

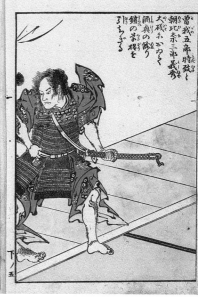

TORII KIYONAGA 1752–1815

17 *Ehon Monomi ga Oka*
   ('Picture-book of Hills of Fair Views')

Illustrated: Entertaining clients on a veranda in the Fudo
   Rakudō district
Published by Nishimura Genroku and Iseya Kichijūrō
2 parts (in 1 vol.), 1785
Woodblock, 222 × 163 mm
Hillier 144

Life in Edo throughout the year as recorded by
one of the foremost *Ukiyoe* artists. About 1850 a
new edition was published in colour, with the
heads recut to bring the style of hairdressing up to
date.

TORII KIYONAGA

18 *Ehon Muchibukuro*
   ('Picture-book of Heroes and Heroines')

Illustrated: The hero Asahina Saburō tugs at the armour of
   Sōga Gorō
Published by Iseya Jinosuke
1 vol., 1782
Woodblock, 217 × 198 mm
OA 129A

The heroes of legend were well known through
the Kabuki theatre and through popular
literature. The usually rather placid Kiyonaga
shows a surprising command of violent
movement in this rare book.

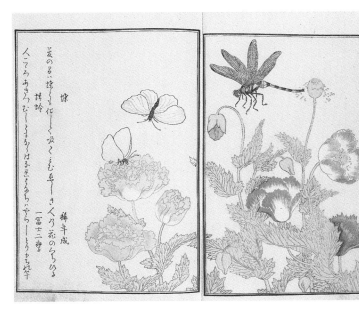

KITAO MASANOBU 1761–1816

19 *Yoshiwara Keisei Shin Bijin Awase Jihitsu Kagami* ('A Mirror Comparing the Handwriting of New and Beautiful Courtesans of the Yoshiwara')

Illustrated: The courtesan Nanasato writing poetry (standing) and Utagawa reading (seated) with attendants
Published by Tsutaya Jūsaburō
1 vol., 1784
Woodblock, 382 × 255 mm
Hillier 146

This is one of the most sumptuously printed of all Japanese colour-printed albums. The seven unusually large prints depict leading courtesans of the day in their finery, with verses inscribed above in their own calligraphy. The sheets are usually found detached and as a result faded, but this fine copy gives full credit to one of the most influential masterpieces of *Ukiyoe* art.

KITAGAWA UTAMARO 1753–1806

20 *Ehon Mushi Erabi* ('Picture-book of Selected Insects')

Illustrated: Dragonfly, butterflies and poppies
Published by Tsutaya Jūsaburō
2 vols, 1788
Woodblock with mica and gauffrage, 271 × 185 mm
Hillier 152

In the year 1788 Utamaro's reputation was established by the publication of masterpieces in two entirely different spheres, the *Uta Makura*, an album of unsurpassed erotic prints, and the *Ehon Mushi Erabi*, a book of *kyōka* (comic verse) and of supremely elegant prints of flowers, insects and other creatures.

KITAGAWA UTAMARO

21 *Ehon Waka Ebisu*
   ('Picture-book of Young Ebisu')

Illustrated: New Year's morning
Published by Tsutaya Jūsaburō
1 vol., 1789
Woodblock with gauffrage and gold and silver leaf,
   259 × 189 mm
Hillier 153

This is one of a series of New Year albums, each of
five colour prints, to which *Kyōgetsubō* and
Ginsekai also belong. The title is not easily
translatable because of a play, or plays, on words.
Ebisu is the popular god most associated with the
New Year, but *Waka* can be 'young' or 'thirty-one
syllable poem'. Broadly the meaning can be
rendered as 'An Anthology of New Year Verse'.
The contents are varied, with two prints
simulating the courtly *Tosa* style, a third the
manner of Moronobu, and the remaining two
being contemporary *Ukiyoe*.

KITAGAWA UTAMARO

22 *Kyōgetsubō* ('The Moon-mad Monk')

Illustrated: The exiled Yukihira on the shore at Suma
Published by Tsutaya Jūsaburō
1 vol., 1789
Woodblock with gauffrage and gold and silver leaf,
   254 × 190 mm
Hillier 154

As in *Waka Ebisu*, several of the five printed plates
adopt the style of earlier masters of other schools –
Tosa in the Yukihira episode (illustrated), Itchō in
a rustic scene, and Kanō in a classical landscape.
The full moon figures in all five prints.

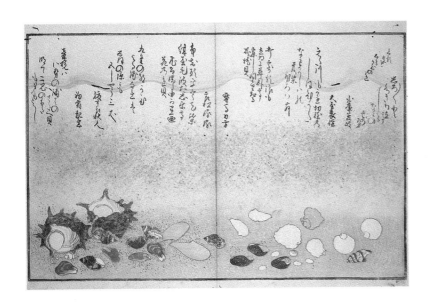

KITAGAWA UTAMARO

23 *Shioi no Tsuto* ('Gifts of the Ebb-tide')

Illustrated: Shells by the shore, illustrating *kyōka* poems
Published by Tsutaya Jūsaburō
1 vol., *c.* 1790
Woodblock with gauffrage, brass dust, mica, gold and
   silver leaf, 260 × 190 mm
Hillier 158

There are eight colour prints: an opening view of
shell-gathering at Shinagawa Bay; six prints of
shells, seaweed and other sea wrack (one
illustrated); and a fine interior scene of women
playing the Shell Game (*kai-awase*). This is the first
issue, with wave lines decorating the upper part
of each page of shells, and scattered brass dust
simulating the sand of the beach. It is
acknowledged as one of the technical
masterpieces of Japanese woodblock printing.

KITAGAWA UTAMARO

24 *Momo Chidori* ('A Hundred Plovers' *or*
        'Hundreds and Thousands of Birds')

Illustrated: Pigeons and sparrows with maple leaves
Published by Tsutaya Jūsaburō
2 vols, *c.* 1791
Woodblock with gauffrage, 255 × 190 mm
OA 141

This is arguably the most stylish of all Utamaro's
books, and the one in which he vindicated his
implied claims to be superior to the contemporary
artists of the official Kanō School, both in delicacy
of execution and originality of design. Like all the
great albums published by Tsutaya, this is a *kyōka*
(comic verse) book, but the power of the
illustrations and printing far outweigh the literary
content.

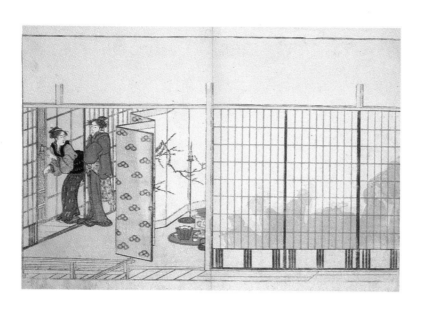

KITAGAWA UTAMARO

25 *Ginsekai* ('The Silver World')

Illustrated: An evening party
Published by Tsutaya Jūsaburō
1 vol., 1790
Woodblock with gauffrage, 255 × 190 mm
Hillier 526

This album, with five snow scenes in a variety of
styles, is one of a traditional trilogy of 'Snow,
Moon and Flowers' (*setsugekka*). *Kyōgetsubō* (no.
22) represents the Moon, and *Fugenzō* (the name
of a cherry variety) the Flowers (no. 26).

KITAGAWA UTAMARO

26 *Fugenzō* ('The Image of Fugen' – the
name of a variety of flowering cherry)

Illustrated: Cherry-blossom viewing on Edo Bay
Published by Tsutaya Jūsaburō
1 vol., 1790
Woodblock with applied gold and gauffrage,
  252 × 182 mm
OA 140A

One of three albums of *kyōka* (comic verse)
designed by Utamaro on the classic set of 'Snow,
Moon, Flowers'; this is the flowers volume, with
illustrations of cherry-viewing in April. The snow
is *Ginsekai* ('The Silver World') and the Moon
Kyōgetsubō ('The Moon-Mad Monk').

KITAGAWA UTAMARO

27 *Seirō Ehon Nenjū Gyōji* ('Picture-book of
     Events of the Year in the Green Houses')

Illustrated: Cleaning up after a riotous spell
Published by Kazusaya Chōsuke
2 vols, 1804
Woodblock, 225 × 158 mm
Hillier 159

The most widely known of Utamaro's books,
partly because a translation of the lively text, by
the comic writer Jippensha Ikku (1765–1831),
figured in Edmond de Goncourt's *Outamaro: Le
Peintre des Maisons Vertes* (Paris, 1896).
The most celebrated page shows a rather idealised
Utamaro decorating the interior of one of the
Houses with a painting of a phoenix, watched by
admiring courtesans.

KATSUKAWA SHUN'EI 1762–1819
with KATSUKAWA SHUNSHŌ 1726–92

28 *Imawa-mukashi* ('Once Upon a Time . . .')

Illustrated: The former wife's return
Published by Suharaya Ichibei, Enshuya Bishichi and
     Sankiya Seikichi
3 vols, 1790
Woodblock, 207 × 148 mm
Hillier 163

A book of ghost stories. The colophon indicates
that Shun'ei was assisted by his master, Shunshō.
This is the most imaginative and the best designed
and printed of all Japanese books of diablerie. The
title is an elaborate play on written characters; the
first three can mean 'stories of strange demons' as
well as 'once upon a time'.

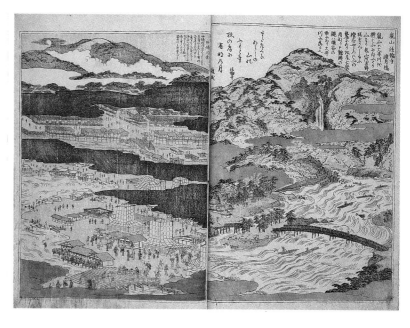

KATSUKAWA SHUNCHŌ
Worked *c.* 1780–1800

29 *Ehon Sakaegusa* ('Picture-book of a
Prosperous Household')

Illustrated: Cooling off by the water in summer
Published by Izumiya Ichibei
2 vols, 1790
Woodblock, 217 × 154 mm
Hillier 496

A woman's life, her schooldays, and wedding in
volume 1; her life after marriage, the birth of a
child, and the first visit to a temple with the child
in volume 2. The books are a sort of guide to
accepted middle-class usage for those aspiring to
that status.

KEISAI MASAYOSHI 1764–1824

30 *Ehon Miyako no Nishiki* ('Picture-book of
Brocades of the Capital')

Illustrated: The Shijō-Kawara river district (left) and the
Togetsukyō Bridge at Arashiyama (right)
Published by Yoshinoya Tamehachi, Kyoto
1 vol., 1787
Woodblock, 300 × 220 mm
Hillier 480

Landscape prints of this amplitude and
complexity had rarely been accomplished before
in Japan. 'Brocades' refer to the coloured
woodblock process, which reproduces in printed
and expanded form the characteristics of *Yamatoe*
(native Japanese) landscape style. Miyako was a
name for Kyoto, which remained the formal
capital until 1867.

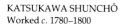

KEISAI MASAYOSHI

31 *Raikin Zui*, vol. I
('Picture Collection of Imported Birds')

Illustrated: Silver pheasants
Published by Matsumoto Zembei
1 vol., 1789
Woodblock with gauffrage, 251 × 187 mm
OA 90

This is apparently one of only two surviving
copies of the first edition of this superb album,
and is the only one which can rival the Tsutaya
Jūsaburō *kyōka* books designed by Utamaro. The
colophon announces two more volumes to follow,
but they do not survive and may not have
appeared at all. Masayoshi 'redesigned' the
originals (whatever they were) of the Nagasaki
artist Ishōsai Shūsen Genyū (1736–1824). The
selection was made by a Chinese, Guan Yingwen.

VARIOUS ARTISTS

32 *Haru no Iro* ('The Colours of Spring')

Illustrated: Utamaro: mirror-polisher with shrine maiden
Published by Tsutaya Jūsaburō
1 vol., 1794
Woodblock, 245 × 187 mm
Hillier 171

This is the earliest of a series of New Year annuals,
published by Tsutaya, consisting of numerous
kyōka (comic poems) supplied by writers of one or
other of the leading clubs, accompanied by five or
six colour prints by leading artists of the day.
Kubo Shumman figures prominently as the
designer of a number of the prints and, as a leader
of the verse-clubs, he seems to have been
something of a guiding spirit in the publication of
these anthologies. In this album the artists are
Unzan and Tōrin (of the Tsutsumi school), Rinshō
(a follower of Hanabusa Itchō and a frequent
collaborator with Shumman), and Utamaro,
Shumman and Shigemasa of the *Ukiyoe* school.

VARIOUS ARTISTS

33 *Momo Saezuri* ('A Hundred Twitterings')

Illustrated: Shumman: ferry over the Sumida River in Edo
Published by Tsutaya Jūsaburō
1 vol., 1796
Woodblock, 258 × 190 mm
Hillier 176a

The prints in this *kyōka* book are by Shōhō, Tōrin (two), Kahō Sambei and Shumman (two, one illustrated).

VARIOUS ARTISTS

34 *Ehon Uta Yomidori* ('Picture-book:
      Poems of Birds of the Four Quarters')

Illustrated: Women celebrating the New Year
Published by Tsutaya Jūsaburō
1 vol., 1795
Woodblock, 255 × 190 mm
Hillier 176

Of the six prints in this *kyōka* (comic verse) album one is a joint work by Tōrin, Shumman and Rinshō; the others are by Tōrin, Shumman (two), Shōhō and Rinshō. The print by Shumman is a masterpiece of *Ukiyoe*, displaying sumptuous and dazzling colour printing.

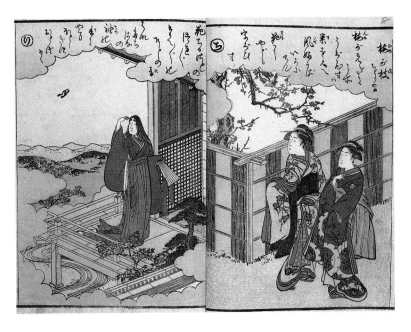

KUBO SHUMMAN 1757–1820 and TŌSHŪ

35 *Yomo no Yama* ('Mountains of the Four Quarters')

Illustrated: Shumman: travesty of a Nō play (possibly
Susano-o and the Princess in *Orochi*)
1 vol., *c.* 1805–10
Woodblock, 195 × 135 mm
Hillier 205

An album of *kyōka* (comic verse) with six
outstanding colour prints in *surimono* style by
Shumman and Tōshū. The prints all illustrate Nō
plays.

(?)EISHŌSAI CHŌKI
Worked late 18th–early 19th centuries

36 *Ehon Matsu no Shirabe* ('Picture-book of the Music of the Pine-trees')

Illustrated: Two contemporary women looking at a
nightingale on a plum branch (right) and the lady
Hanachirusato from *The Tale of Genji* standing on a
veranda (left).
Published by Tsutaya Jūsaburō
1 vol., preface dated 1795
Woodblock, 240 × 170 mm
Hillier 495

The pictures illustrate the verses of four songs for
koto music and the incidents which gave rise to
them; the title comes from the comparison of the
sounds of this instrument to the wind passing
through pine-trees.

HOSODA EISHI 1756–1829

37 *Ehon Kasen Shū* ('Picture-book Collection of Immortal Poets')

Illustrated: The classic poets Shigeyuki (left) and Toshiyuki (right) with women in late 18th-century dress
Published by Nishimuraya Yohachi (Eijūdō)
1 vol., 1799
Woodblock, 253 × 218 mm
Hillier 181

Inside the front cover is a print of an *uguisu* (nightingale) on a flowering plum; then follow thirty-six single-page prints, each depicting one of the classic 'Thirty-six Poets', accompanied by two, usually female, attendants in contemporary *Ukiyoe* style, with a verse of the poet above a conventional cloud line. The style and the restrained colour have much in common with the Genji triptychs designed a few years earlier by Eishi (nos 114–15). Very few copies have been recorded.

VARIOUS ARTISTS

38 *Otoko-dōka* ('The Men's Stamping Song')

Illustrated: Eishi: a grand courtesan with her attendants in the Shin Yoshiwara licensed district on New Year's morning
Published by Tsutaya Jūsaburō
1 vol., 1798
Woodblock, 255 × 185 mm
Hillier 156

The title is the name of a men's dance performed on the fifteenth day of the first month, and hence implies the New Year. This was the last of the series of splendid *kyōka* (comic verse) albums published under the imprint of Tsutaya, who had died in 1797. The artists were Shigemasa, Ekiji, Eishi (illustrated), Hokusai, Tōrin and Utamaro, whose print of women on the veranda of a house has been frequently reproduced in Western literature on the artist.

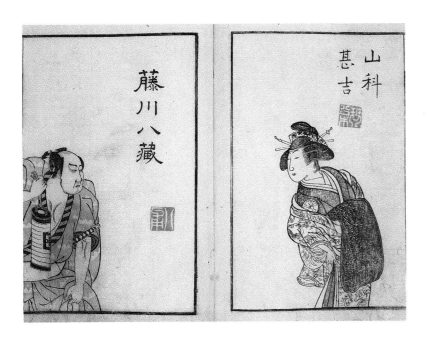

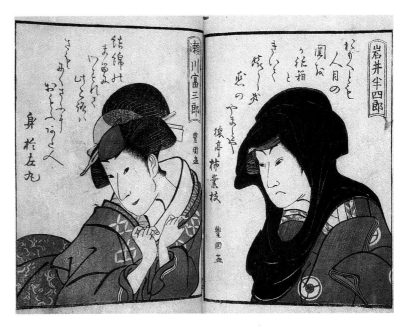

KUNITAKA SUIFUTEI
Worked 1780s

39 *Suifutei Gigafu* ('An Album
of Humorous Pictures by Suifutei')

Illustrated: The Kabuki actors Fujikawa Hachizō (left) and
   Yamashina Jinkichi (right)
Published by Seikōdō, probably Osaka
1 vol., 1782
Woodblock, 260 × 160 mm
Hillier 139

These highly individual portraits of actors are
remarkable for their extreme asymmetry of
placement on the page. They seem to have had a
profound influence on the Western Japanese
school of actor portraitists, especially Ryūkōsai
and Shōkōsai.

UTAGAWA TOYOKUNI 1769–1825
UTAGAWA KUNIMASA 1773–1810

40 *(Nigao Ehon) Yakusha Gakuya Tsū*
('Portrait Picture-book of Actors in their
Dressing-rooms')

Illustrated: The Kabuki actors Segawa Tomosaburō (left)
   and Iwai Hanshirō (right)
Published by Kazusaya Chūsuke
1 vol., preface dated 1799
Woodblock, 182 × 128 mm
Hillier 160

There is also a double-page frontispiece of
theatre-goers in the foyer of a theatre by Utamaro
and a single-page print of theatrical mask-costume
for the *sambasō* dance, unsigned. The thirty-six
half-length portraits of actors are by Toyokuni and
Kunimasa, each with a *kyōka* (comic verse)
inscribed in the background.

UTAGAWA TOYOKUNI

41 *Yakusha Sangaikyō* ('Amusements of
   Actors on the Third Floor')

Illustrated: Actors of the Ichikawa family on their own
   river-boat, with colleagues as guests
Published by Shunshōken Nishimiya Shinroku and
   Yorozuya Tajiemon
2 vols, 1801
Woodblock, 218 × 156 mm
Hillier 196

The private lives of entertainers were of deep
interest to the public, and this very finely printed
work, its designs often appropriately dramatic,
served as a superior sort of gossip-sheet. The
'third floor' housed the actors' dressing-rooms.

UTAGAWA TOYOKUNI 1769–1825

42 *Ehon Imayo Sugata* ('Picture-book of
   Modern Figures of Fashion')

Illustrated: Geisha preparing a Niwaka Festival
   performance
Published by Izumiya Ichibei (Kansendō)
2 vols, 1802
Woodblock, 217 × 145 mm
Hillier 194

The first volume depicts women in general, from
court ladies to farmers' wives; the second centres
on women of the licensed quarters. In the first
edition the cartouches alongside each figure gave
their names, but soon after the first issue, for
reasons that have never been established, the
names were removed, leaving blanks (as in the
pages displayed). This work is distinguished for
its lively and detailed view of contemporary life
and for its covers, beautifully embossed with the
artist's seals.

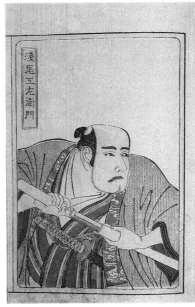

UTAGAWA TOYOKUNI

43 *Yakusha Awase Kagami*
   ('A Mirror of Actors Compared')

Illustrated: Kabuki actors of the Iwai family (left) and
   Ichikawa family (right)
Published by Banshundō and Yamadaya Sanshirō
2 vols, 1804
Woodblock, 267 × 181 mm
Hillier 200

One of the outstanding books devoted to Kabuki
actors, here depicted half-length in the style in
which Toyokuni scored some of his most striking
successes in single-sheet form. The preservation
of the colours in this copy is remarkable.

SHŌKŌSAI HAMBEI
Worked *c.* 1795–1809

44 *Santo Yakusha Masukagami* ('A Clear
   Mirror of Actors of the Three Cities')

Illustrated: The Kabuki actors Asao Kuzaemon (left) and
   Kyōminshi (right)
Published by Shioya Chōbei, Osaka
2 vols, 1806
Woodblock, 219 × 153 mm
Hillier 212

Hokushū, a major Osaka designer of actor prints,
shows in this book how much he owed to
Toyokuni, especially *Yakusha Awase Kagami* ('A
Mirror of Actors Compared'), published two years
earlier (no. 43). The 'Three Cities' are Edo, Osaka
and Kyoto.

KATSUSHIKA HOKUSAI 1760–1849
KITAO SHIGEMASA 1739–1820

45 *Miyama Uguisu*
   ('Nightingale in the Mountains')

Illustrated: Plum bough
No publisher given, but probably Edo
1 vol., *c.* 1798
Woodblock, 195 × 132 mm
Hillier 410

Hokusai and Shigemasa each contributed a single
print. Hokusai's (illustrated) is signed 'Hokusai
Sōri after a painting by Hokkyō Kōrin' (Ogata
Kōrin, 1652–1716), and is on paper minutely
embossed to suggest a silk weave.

KATSUSHIKA HOKUSAI 1760–1849

46 *Tarōtsuki*
   ('The First Moon' or 'The Moon of Tarō')

Illustrated: Scene from a *kyōgen* drama, with Tarō holding
   an umbrella
No publisher given, but probably Edo
1 vol., *c.* 1797–8
Woodblock, 225 × 165 mm
Hillier 412

A book of *kyōka* (comic verse) with a single colour
print signed Sōri. Tarō is the name of a *kyōgen*
drama character who appears in the print in this
book.

KATSUSHIKA HOKUSAI

47 Untitled album

Illustrated: Peasants by a shrine on the Sumida River in
Edo, with Mt Fuji in the distance
No publisher given, but probably Edo
1 vol., 1796
Woodblock, 205 × 140 mm
Hillier 406

A rare, perhaps unique, *kyōka* (comic verse) book
with a four-page *surimono*-style print, which
rather unusually folds out flat, of peasants on the
bank of the Sumida River with great pine-trees in
the foreground (illustrated); and two single-sheet
prints, one of peonies, the other of a cuckoo flying
above herbage. The cover is embossed and
colour-printed with chrysanthemums.

KATSUSHIKA HOKUSAI

48 *Tōto Shōkei Ichiran* ('Fine Views of the Eastern Capital at a Glance')

Illustrated: Hostesses see off clients from an establishment
on the Sumida River
Published by Suharaya Mohei, Suharaya Ihachi and
Tsutaya Jūsaburō
2 vols, 1800
Woodblock, 260 × 170 mm
Hillier 438

This is the first of three major sets of books by
Hokusai depicting the sights of Edo in colour
prints, to which the accompanying *kyōka* ('comic
verse') are quite subsidiary.

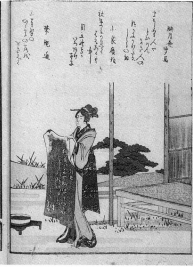

KATSUSHIKA HOKUSAI

49 *Ehon Kyōka Yama Mata Yama*
('Picture-book of Kyōka:
Mountains upon Mountains')

Illustrated: Priest taking ink rubbings from a stone
monument in Edo.
Published by Tsutaya Jūsaburō
3 vols, 1804
Woodblock, 264 × 175 mm
Hillier 440

Despite the title, the pictures relate only to the
slightly hilly north and north-western areas of
Edo.

KATSUSHIKA HOKUSAI

50 *Hokusai Soga* ('Sketches by Hokusai')

Illustrated: 'Wintry blast'
Published by Eirakuya, Nagoya, with Suharaya Mohei
and seven others in Edo (according to the colophon in
coloured edition)
1 vol., 1820
Woodblock, 255 × 180 mm
Hillier 449

A rather superior form of *Manga* ('ten-thousand
sketches') miscellany. Two editions exist, one in
ink only, another with pink and grey tints.

KATSUSHIKA HOKUSAI

51 *Fugaku Hyakkei*
(‘One Hundred Views of Fuji’)

Illustrated: Fuji from the umbrella-makers’ in Aoyama
(left) and from the edge of a village (right)
Published by Eirakuya Tōjirō, Nagoya (main publisher)
3 vols, dated 1834, 1835, *c.* 1849
Woodblock, 227 × 157 mm
Hillier 454

Acknowledged as one of the supreme illustrated
books of Japan and, together with his *Manga*, the
most influential in the West. The first editions of
each of the first two volumes, because of title-slips
printed with a falcon’s feather, are known as the
‘Falcon Feather’ editions. The third volume,
issued much later by a different publisher, does
not match the earlier volumes in refinement of
black and white printing.

YASHIMA GAKUTEI *c.* 1786–1868

52 *Ichirō Gafu* (‘Ichirō’s Picture-album’)

Illustrated: Autumn landscape
Published by Gasendō
1 vol., 1823
Woodblock with gauffrage, 227 × 158 mm
Hillier 274

Ichirō was one of Gakutei’s art-names. The prints
appeared first in a privately published *kyōka*
(comic verse) book in two volumes entitled
Sansui Kikan Kyōka-shū (‘Collected *kyōka* and
Landscapes of Strange Sights’), undated but
c. 1820. This publication shows the continuing
vitality of the tradition of *kyōka* illustration in the
woodblock book.

YASHIMA GAKUTEI
UTAGAWA KUNISADA 1786–1864
and a pupil of Kunisada

53 *Uta no Tomobune*
   ('A Friends' Boat of Verses')

Illustrated: Kunisada: under the Ryōgoku Bridge in Edo
No publisher given, but Edo
3 vols, *c.* 1830
Woodblock, 225 × 152 mm
Hillier 559

This is a set of volumes privately printed for the
Hommachi *kyōka* (comic verse) society of Edo.
One volume is illustrated by each of the three
artists, for the third of whom there is no
signature. The landscapes of Gakutei are
remarkable for their manneristic treatment and
the subtle use of the colour-print medium.
Kunisada's view of boats under the Ryōgoku
Bridge is reproduced here.

TOTOYA HOKKEI 1780–1850

54 *Sansai Hana Hyakushū*
   Sansai Tsuki Hyakushū
   Sansai Yuki Hyakushū
   ('Three Aspects of (1) Flowers, (2) Moon,
   (3) Snow in a Collection of
   One Hundred Verses')

Illustrated: Cherry-blossom by a stream
Published by Shunyūtei
3 vols, 1828–30
Woodblock, 225 × 160 mm
Hillier 293

A set of three *kyōka* (comic verse) anthologies,
based on the classical trilogy, 'Snow, Moon and
Flowers' (*setsugekka*), each with three colour
prints. The *Sansai* of the title derives from Chinese
philosophy and implies the separate principles of
Heaven, Earth and Man. Thus all three prints in
each book obliquely relate to Heaven, Earth and
Man: for example, in the 'Moon' volume Heaven
is invoked by the moon in a pine-tree; Earth, by
plovers flying over waves; and Man, by a figure in
an autumn field.

YANAGAWA SHIGENOBU 1787–1832

55 *Kyōka Meisho Zue*
   ('Kyōka Illustrated with Fine Views')

Illustrated: View at Fuji Musashino
No publisher given, but possibly Edo
1 vol., 1826
Woodblock, 228 × 161 mm
Hillier 284

ANDŌ HIROSHIGE 1797–1858

56 *Kyōka Yamato Jimbutsu*
   ('National Types in Comic Verse')

Illustrated: Streetwalkers (left) and abalone fishers (right)
No publisher given, but probably Edo
7 vols, mid 1850s
Woodblock, 234 × 166 mm
Hillier 351

The verses are on the theme of trades and
professions, and give Hiroshige opportunities for
humorous figure drawings which are printed in
light colours. The covers of the volumes are
noteworthy for their decorations of dragon-flies in
gold on blue. Although this set of volumes is
undated, dates of 1855 and 1857 are quoted in
Japanese sources.

UTAGAWA KUNISADA 1786–1864 TOTOYA HOKKEI 1780–1850

57 *Yakusha Sanjū-rokkasen* ('A Selection of Thirty-six Flowers of the Acting Profession')

Illustrated: Kunisada: portraits of Kabuki actors, accompanied by *haiku* poems
Published by Nishimuraya Yōhachi and Nakamuraya Katsugōrō
1 vol. (of three), 1835
Woodblock, 255 × 185 mm
Hillier 331

The portraits of actors are by Kunisada (illustrated). Hokkei provided three views, each of a famous landmark. The title is a pun on the anthology of 'Thirty-six Poets' made in the Middle Ages and known to every educated Japanese. This copy is one volume of the original three.

GOUNTEI SADAHIDE 1807–73

58 *Yokohama Kaikō Kembun Shi* ('An Account of the Opening of the Port of Yokohama')

Illustrated: Foreign sailors drunk in the main street of Yokohama
No publisher given, but Edo
2 vols, 1862
Woodblock, 245 × 177 mm
Hillier 364

In this book Sadahide illustrates the establishment of the Western presence in Japan and also gives pictures, imaginary or based on Western originals, of the Western world. Sadahide is unquestionably the most gifted of the numerous Japanese artists who reported pictorially this crucial period in the country's history. Their work in sheet-print form is known as *Yokohamae* (pictures of, not produced in, Yokohama).

KAWANABE GYŌSAI 1831–89

59 *Kyōsai Gafu* ('Kyōsai's Picture-album')

Illustrated: Octopus turning the tables on fishmongers (left); scholar's head stuck in a bronze vessel (right)
Published by Kinkadō, Tokyo
1 vol., 1880
Woodblock, 228 × 160 mm
Hillier 379

Kyōsai, confusingly, was an art-name of Gyōsai, and he is often known by it. This turbulent post-Edo artist can claim to be Hokusai's true artistic successor, although he had no direct connections with him.

58

57

59